A Bloodstained Hammer

A Story from the Kootenays

Alison Townsend and Brian T. Seifrit

Published by

Copyright © 2010 – 2020
Alison Townsend and Brian T. Seifrit

ISBN: 978-1-7773280-8-5 Print Book
ISBN: 978-1-7773280-9-2 eBook

The story is a fictionalized description based on the *actual Townsend murders* that occurred in the outskirts of Fruitvale, British Columbia in 1959. The conversations, thoughts expressed and activities are the product of the authors' imaginations. The first name of the surviving victims and the last name of the accused have been changed

.

Chapter 1

The letter arrived in early September just before the hog-harvesting season. Kent Townsend picked it up and looked it over, then tossed it back on the counter. He was hoping it was a response to his ad for a farm hand. Kent had tried keeping the farm up on his own, but with working at Cominco full-time, he found it extremely hard and exhausting to come home to hours of chores. Right now, he had no time to look at the letter, there were thirty hogs that needed feeding and they were letting him know that he was late, with their unrelenting squealing.

"Damn hogs, I'm on my way," he said, annoyed at their persistence. He put on his boots and jacket and stepped out into the evening air. The chilly evening was nature's way of saying that fall was fast approaching. The family dog ran up to him as he made his way to the hog barn.

"Well, hello there, old girl. How are you today?" The dog pranced ahead scaring a few chickens away as Kent opened the barnyard gate. He walked to the barn where the hog feed was kept, and checked the rabbit cage. He wanted to make sure that the rabbits were watered and fed. It was his daughter and oldest son's job, although they were not quite old enough for him to expect that they would do it every day, he wanted to ensure it was. He smiled as he noted how clean the cage was. *Looks like the kids did their chores today,* he thought as he reached for the first sack of hog feed. Tossing it over his shoulder, he carried it to the wheelbarrow outside. The second sack he lifted did not seem to be as light as the first, and it hurt his back as he swung it over his shoulder.

"I'm getting too old for this. Sure hope that letter is a reply from someone looking for work," he said quietly to himself as he made his way to the wheelbarrow with the second sack.

The dog sat patiently by, and he looked at her. "One more to go and that will do it for the hogs tonight." With the third sack loaded up, he paused for a minute to catch his breath, and then with some effort, wheeled the feed to the hog barn. By now, the hogs were aware of him and once again started with their squealing. Opening the barn door, he hollered at them. "Shut up piggies, shut up! Food is on its way!"

Oddly, silence filled the barn. The hogs understood it when he yelled at them. "That's better. Now I can enjoy some silence without all your snorting and squealing. I could hear you all the way up to the house. I might be a little late, but I'm here now." Chuckling to himself he turned on the water hose and started mixing the hog feed into the ten buckets he used to feed them.

With the final bucket mixed, he loaded them onto the wooden wagon that he made to haul the feed up and down the barn alley. When he dumped the last bucket into the trough of the last stall, he noted that the hog stalls were in need of a cleaning it was a job that, he would have to do on the weekend. "Looks like you hogs got my work cut out for me. Thanks for that," he said, sarcastically.

Whistling, he made his way back to the barn foyer and cleaned the buckets for next time. The evening was colder than usual, so he fired up the wood-burning boiler to pump some heat into the cold, dank barn. The last thing he needed was for the hogs to get sick. He had thirty of them, and at a cost of $10.00 each, it was a $300.00 investment.

Losing any of them to illness was always a worry. He had switched them over to a 5% higher fiber intake at the beginning of the year. According to the experts, the higher fiber content would help the hogs fight off certain viral illnesses. So far, it was working and the hogs were putting on weight nicely, none of them was sick, and that was always a plus. Puffing on his pipe, he thought about this while the barn warmed up. Tossing a few more logs into the boiler, he turned down the damper, shut off the light, and headed back to the house. A sunset to the west caught his eye, and he whistled a happy tune as he made his way to a well deserved, supper.

His wife Sylvia was setting the table. She was beautiful in his eyes. With her long, charcoal-black hair and dark chocolate brown eyes, she made him realize how lucky he was every time he looked at her. Their children Emily, age eight, and Richard, age five sat at their usual spots at the table. Their youngest boy, Jack, age two, sat in the highchair next to his mother. Poking his head into the dining room, he asked Emily if she and Richard had washed up for dinner. Emily nodded that they had.

"Good. Because we don't want dirty hands around the dinner table, do we?" He had always been adamant about that. He went to the bathroom himself to wash up. After scrubbing his hands and face, he looked in the mirror and stroked his whiskered chin. *Maybe I should have a shave,* he thought as he dried his hands. The smell of Sylvia's cooking wafted towards him. It made his mouth water and his stomach growl. *Nah, dinner first shave later,* he decided.

Right from the beginning, Sylvia had been an excellent cook. Her mother had taught her well. Sitting at the head of the table Kent winked at his children and then poked his daughter in the ribs. "How was school today?"

"It was okay, but I don't like the boy who sits next to me."

"Why is that?" he asked, with concern.

"He keeps making funny faces at me. Like this," Emily put her fingers in her ears and went cross-eyed sticking out her tongue. "Just like that, all the time."

Kent chuckled, "It looks to me that he is only teasing you. I wouldn't worry about it."

"But Dad, I don't want to look at his ugly tongue, and he looks so stupid when he goes cross-eyed. Yuk."

"Don't pay any attention to him Emily," her mother interjected. "Boys will be boys, and even the older ones are gross sometimes." She looked over to Kent, "take a look at your father with all those yucky whiskers. He looks so much better when he's shaved," she teased as she sat down.

"There are only so many hours in a day, and until Ricky and Jack are big enough to help me out with the chores, I might never have the time to shave again," Kent jokingly replied. This time he winked at his boys.

"I'm almost old enough aren't I?" Richard asked. "I don't want you to have a hairy face like Uncle Willard, no way!"

"I'll tell you what, you, come down to the barn with me tomorrow night when I do the chores. If you can dump a bucket of slop without spilling any, you're old enough, and I'll shave," he smiled at the young boy and nodded, "now let's eat. I am as hungry as the hogs, and we don't want your mother's cooking getting any colder. Come on, let's eat up." He scooped out potatoes and Salisbury gravy onto his children's plates while their mother handed out the Salisbury steak and biscuits. "You've outdone yourself again darling," Kent remarked as he looked at his wife.

"We'll have something else tomorrow night. I didn't get to town today to pick anything up."

"That's all right, I don't mind hamburger steak. What about you Richard, Emmy; do the two of you mind hamburger steak?" He looked at them waiting for their reply.

"No, sir," they replied in unison. They knew better than to complain about the food.

"See Sylvia, we don't mind Salisbury steak at all." It was quiet around the table as they ate their meal. Kent broke the silence by asking the children about their day. "So, Emily had a good day at school. What about you Richard, how was your day?"

"I cleaned the rabbit cage all by myself," he said, with enthusiasm. Richard always wanted to be like his father. To work hard meant that you were growing up. Although he was only five, he seemed to know more than most five year olds. Taking another mouthful of food, he chewed and then continued. "Then I went down to the creek and caught a frog. Mom told me to put it back. She doesn't like frogs."

"Of course she doesn't. She's a girl, and girls don't like frogs," Emily responded.

Kent and Sylvia both laughed.

"There is nothing wrong with frogs; in fact, they taste good."

"Oh Kent, please, we're eating," Sylvia waved her hand through the air.

"Ooohhh, Daddy that is gross," Emily rolled her eyes.

"I was only teasing. It's their legs that taste good, not the whole frog," he chuckled.

"Do you really eat frog legs?" Richard asked.

"No, son, I was only making fun. The French though eat them all the time. They eat the giant bullfrogs with fat legs. If you find any bullfrogs, we might sell them to the French." Kent smiled at his son and winked. "That is enough talking for now, eat up."

"Thank God," Sylvia put some potatoes on a spoon for Jack, who wrinkled up his nose. "What is the matter Jack, don't you like potatoes?" She wiped his chin with a napkin, and he fought the whole time. "All right, that is enough. I guess he doesn't want any more. Emily will you please get Jack his sippy-cup with some apple juice in it. I would get it, but his supper is everywhere. He needs to wash down these potatoes. I think this little fellow should have a bath tonight too." Sylvia rose from the table and took Jack out of his high chair. "We'll put you in your baby seat and your sister will give you some juice. Emily where is Jack's juice?"

"Coming Mom, I wanted to rinse it out. Here it is Jack." She handed Jack the sippy-cup, and he took it in his hands and began to drink. "He sure likes his juice, doesn't he," Emily smiled, she loved her brothers and was the mothering type, always looking out for the two of them like big sisters do.

"He sure does Emily. I only wish he had eaten a bit more. Nevertheless, I guess he is done. Now hurry up and finish your dinner, so you can help me with the dishes."

"Yes Mom," Emily darted back to the table.

"Whoa, slow down little girl, you almost bumped the table and spilled your milk."

"Sorry Dad."

"That's all right. Just be careful. Now finish up your dinner." Kent took the last mouthful of food that was on his plate, rose from the table, and poured a coffee. Retrieving the letter that he picked up that day on his way home from work, he sat down in his favorite chair, and set his coffee on the end table. He opened the envelope and began to read the letter.

"Is it a letter from someone who answered your ad?" Sylvia questioned as she began to clear the table.

"It sure is. It is from a fellow named Alex Hudulak. According to the letter, he has experience. He is a good prospect, is young and single. It says he has worked for a few different ranches and farms up North."

"Is there a number where you can reach him?"

"Nope, only an address, I guess I will send him a note. If he is still interested, I think I will hire him. He's got good credentials."

"It is up to you. I know you need help."

"That is an understatement. I am working ten to twelve hours a day up at the smelter and coming home to all those dang hogs. It makes a man tired you know."

"I won't argue about that. I think the extra help will be a Godsend. I say send him a letter, and get him here as soon as possible. Butchering season is around the corner, and you are certainly going to need the help. There aren't many young men around here that would help for a day or two while we harvest the hogs. Besides, we need a good hired hand to help with all the other things too."

Sylvia and Emily continued to wash the dishes. Kent reached over to the end table and grabbed a note pad. He scribbled out a return letter offering the job and a decent wage of $2.25 per hour plus room and board.

"There, that takes care of that. Have we got any envelopes?"

"There should be a box in our Christmas stuff. I use them to send Christmas cards, but I'm sure they'll work the same to send a letter."

"I don't want to use colored envelopes. Don't we have any plain white ones?"

"You are so fussy. I honestly don't think it will matter, if you use one of them."

"I'm not going to use a frilly envelope to send a man a letter of employment. I'll pick one up on my way home from work tomorrow."

"Suit yourself I guess," she replied as she scooped the leftovers from the plates into the dog's dish.

"Emily, the rest of those leftovers can go into this container. We'll have them for lunch on Saturday," she handed her daughter an empty lard container with a lid.

With the supper dishes now out of the way, she poured herself a coffee and sat next to Kent on the couch.

"I was thinking…" she began.

"Oh oh, what were you thinking?" Kent interrupted as he looked at her and winked.

"I was thinking that tomorrow the boys, and I would go into town when Emily is in school and do some shopping. I need a few things, and there is a super sale going on at Woolworths in Trail," she took a sip of her coffee.

"Need some money do you?"

"I have a little bit, but it would be nice to have more."

"I don't get paid until the end of next week. You could use the money we have saved in the coffee can if it is that important."

"What, the house money? I do not want to use that. That is for dire emergencies."

Kent tapped out his pipe and refilled it.

"We'll call it an emergency, how is that? Just make sure you count it right down to the nickel."

He brought a match up to the pipe and puffed until it glowed. The sweet scent of pipe tobacco filled the room, and he smiled. He always enjoyed his pipe.

"Besides, I don't think you have bought yourself anything new in a long while," he leaned in close to her and whispered, "and I'm getting tired of hamburger…" Leaning back, he smiled and took a long puff from his pipe.

"That's the emergency."

There was a glint of contentment in his eye.

"I'll replace whatever money you use from the house money, don't worry about that."

"Really, you don't mind?" Sylvia felt reluctant.

"No, not at all, we need things, and that is what the money is for."

Sylvia now leaned in close to him and kissed him on the cheek. "Thank you, Kent. Thank you so much."

"No, no, thank you for giving me such a sweet kiss." He smiled at her, and for a moment reminisced about the first time, he laid eyes on her. He was fresh out of the war, had fought in Italy with the 1st Infantry, and expected to marry the woman he left behind. He was excited about coming home to be back with the one he loved. The war was a horrific experience, and it was her love that would help him heal. Sadly, when he returned he found that she had already married. Devastated at first he soon concluded, that she wasn't who he thought her to be. He was never down for long, and the smile was soon back gracing his lips. He was grateful at that point that they had not married her. Any woman that fickle was not worth the trouble.

One day while he was working odd jobs with an acquaintance, he met Sylvia. Her chocolate brown eyes caught his attention. He was instantly smitten with her. The way she moved was fluid, graceful, and effortless. When she looked at him and smiled, her eyes shone like bright stars in the night sky. Eventually, he got up the nerve to have a conversation with her, and the next thing he knew they started courting. They were soon married and were the perfect couple, and a joy to be around. Always joking and laughing with each other. It was a love that comes only once in a lifetime, and they were lucky enough to have found that love in one another.

In 1951, they moved to Trail, B.C., and found a nice little house to rent. He was lucky in his job search and started working for Cominco almost immediately. His job as a blacksmith in Alberta was not steady enough for him, now that he had a wife to support, and he and Sylvia agreed on moving to the Kootenays. They saved diligently for the next few years knowing they wanted a little piece of land outside Trail. They eventually found a suitable farm in Parksiding, and with all the money they had saved bought a little piece of valley paradise.

They had dreamed and talked about buying a small farm, and now it was a reality. It had a quaint, two bedroom house that was the right size for the two of them. The way it nestled into the hillside was perfect. Trees surrounding the backside of the house were enchanting. It was as if they welcomed the little house to come sit with them. The garden was the envy to all the neighbors, and the pastures were the right size for the little farm that they knew they could manage. Kent sighed as he thought about it all. Sure, they had their difficulties, and money was always tight, but for ten years, they endured all the ups, and downs. Even when their first daughter got ill and passed away, as hard as it was, they survived.

Their second and third daughters were stillborn, and the couple began to feel that their time together was over. They blamed each other for the deaths. They would go days without speaking to one another. It was a devastating time, but, like all the other hardships they faced together in their journey of life, they eventually worked it out, and their love grew that much stronger. They now had Emily, Richard, and Jack. Kent looked over to Sylvia and smiled. He realized that all the things he could want, he already had.

Kent rose from his chair. "Can I get you another coffee?" he asked Sylvia.

"No, thank you, but, you could put the kettle on for me. I have to warm a bottle for Jack. While the bottle is warming, I'll give him a bath."

"All right, where did Emily and Richard get to?" he asked as he made his way into the kitchen.

"They're playing in their room."

"Emily, Richard," he called out. "Do you two want cocoa? I'm putting the kettle on for your mom. If you want cocoa let me know." He turned on the tap, filled the kettle, and then set it on the stove to boil. Emily and Richard came into the kitchen.

"Yes please, Daddy, we would like some cocoa," they said.

"Good, I put enough water in the kettle."

"Will you call us when it is ready?"

"Of course I will Emily. Now go ahead and play with your brother some more. The cocoa will be ready in a few minutes. Then we'll all sit down, and I'll play us some songs on the harmonica before bed, how does that sound?"

"Will you play 'Camp Town Ladies'? I like that song."

"If that is what you'd like to hear, I sure will. Now go on, go play some more." Kent winked at them as he scooted them off. The two children ran back to their bedroom in a whirr of laughs and giggles. With a fresh cup of coffee, he sat down at the kitchen table and looked out the window. Fall was certainly on its way. The trees were an array of reds and oranges. He looked at them intently as the last bit of daylight faded into darkness.

His mind raced with all the farm work ahead of him. The barn stalls needed cleaning, the hogs needed butchering, and fences needed mending. The list seemed to be never ending. He inhaled deeply, sipping from the cup of coffee in his hand. Indeed, there was a lot of work running the farm, but he wouldn't want it any other way. The sound of the boiling kettle brought him back to the here and now.

"Sylvia, the kettle is boiling." He was tired he had worked too many long days over the past week, and didn't have the energy to get up.

"Can you shut it off for me? I'm giving Jack his bath," she called from the bathroom.

Kent set his cup down and rose from the table. "Yep, I'll get it," he shut the stove off, and called Richard and Emily to come and get their cocoa. Emily arrived first. Kent scratched the top of his head as though somewhat confused and looked at her. "Sweetie, can you tell me how much of this stuff I need to put into your cups? I don't have my reading glasses, and the damn writing is so small."

"Daddy! You swore," Emily said with authority. "You're lucky mommy didn't hear you, shame on you."

"I didn't swear," he thought for a moment. "Okay, maybe I did say a naughty word that shouldn't be repeated. Sorry, Emily you are right." Kent handed her the can of cocoa, "How many spoons of cocoa do I need for your drinks?"

Emily was looking at him shaking her head. "Silly Daddy, mommy always puts in four little spoons."

Kent took that as a means to continue teasing his daughter. "Where do we get these little spoons?"

"In the drawer, behind you," Emily was standing there with her hands on her hips, rolling her eyes at him. Kent turned and opened the drawer. Taking out eight little spoons, he put four in each of their cups. Then turned and looked at Emily again. Her hands were still on her hips, but this time she was also tapping her foot on the floor and shaking her head.

11

"What's the matter? You said four little spoons in each," Kent was smiling at her. "That is what I did; I put four little spoons in your cups. See," he held one of the cups up for her to see.

Richard came darting around the corner. He slid across the floor on his feet, stopping short of Emily. There was a look of bewilderment on his face. Wondering why there were four spoons in two cups. He pointed at the cups as if it were the strangest thing he ever saw.

"What's that?"

"It is your cocoa." Kent tried to say it with a straight face.

Richard looked at him in shock and shook his head in confusion. Kent could not help himself at that point and began to laugh. Meanwhile, Emily already had enough of her dad's joke.

"Are you done, Daddy?" she questioned matter-of-factly.

"Nope, forgot to add the water," he could contain himself no longer, and for a few seconds he laughed a little harder and a little louder than usual. "All right, all right, enough of the jokes. The water is cool enough now for the two of you to have your cocoa. Go ahead and sit down. I'll bring it to you."

By the time he got their drinks ready, Sylvia and Jack met them at the table. Jack was bundled up in a cozy sleeper and glowing. He was clean and happy with a big smile across his face. He knew it was time for a warm bottle and a piece of toast. He sat content and listened to the voices of the ones he loved. It was times like this when time stood still.

Chapter 2

By the time the sun rose the next morning, Kent was sitting at the kitchen table with his first cup of coffee and a plate of eggs. It was 5:00 a.m. He was glad it was Friday. It had been a long week, made even longer by the extra hours of work that, he had picked up. Thankfully, today would be the last twelve-hour shift he would have to do for a couple of weeks.

Once Monday rolled around, he would be back on the clock from 7:00 a.m., until 3:30 p.m. How sweet it would be to have those few extra hours in a day to work around the farm. He always looked forward to that. He checked the kitchen clock. It was time to get a move on if he wanted to get to work by 6:00 a.m.

Standing up as quietly as possible, so as not to wake anyone. He pushed in his chair and set his coffee mug and plate in the sink. He grabbed his work jacket, slipped on his boots, and left the warmth of the house to discover a chilly morning. Frost on his truck windows told him how cold the night had been. He scraped them clean, and fired the truck up. Letting it cough and sputter for a few minutes, he walked to the barn to check on his hogs, making sure they had enough leftover slop from the night before to get them through the day. Sylvia, he knew, would give them a sack or two at midday, if needed. Satisfied that the hogs would make it through the day, he headed back to his truck, then off to work.

He always liked the early morning drive. It was a time when he could contemplate the past day's events, and make plans for the next. It dawned on him that he had forgotten the letter he planned to send.

Damn, forgot the letter. I'd best turn around, I guess. The sooner I mail that letter the better.

Slowing to a snail's pace, he made sure the road was clear. Then did a U-turn in the middle of the dirt road and headed back to the house. Ten minutes later he was on the road again, the letter tucked neatly between the seats. By now, Sylvia and the kids were waking up. Emily was brushing her teeth and washing her face, getting ready for school, as her mom made some oatmeal. Jack was sitting in his highchair, babbling away.

"What is it Jack? Is my little man getting hungry?" Sylvia asked.

"No, he's just talking to me, Mom," Richard tossed in as he pulled up to the table. "Will we go into town today?"

"We sure will, as soon as we get Emily off to school."

"I can't wait until I can start school."

"Another year and you'll be riding the bus with your sister."

"I know, but I want to start school now."

Sylvia smiled as she stirred the oatmeal. Richard, she thought, always wanted to learn new things. He was curious as a barn cat; there was no doubt about that.

"You are so inquisitive, Ricky."

"What does that mean?"

"It means, little brother that you are very curious all the time," Emily said as she brought him a bowl of oatmeal.

"Just like Curious George?" he asked as he poured milk into his hot porridge. "Curious George is always getting into trouble. Am I always going to get into trouble?"

"Not at all, it means you like to learn things." Sylvia now sat down with her coffee and toast.

"Yeah, and he has a whole lifetime of learning, like us right Mommy?" Emily added as she sat down.

"Yes, that is right. Your father always says it is good to learn something new every day." She took a sip of her coffee as the children began eating their breakfast.

"I learned yesterday that mommy doesn't like frogs." Richard chuckled, and Jack seemed to understand as he too began to laugh that cute baby laugh of his.

Sylvia smiled, and Emily rolled her eyes. "It isn't only mommy who doesn't like frogs though. I don't like them either Richard."

Richard stayed silent for a moment thinking of something to retort. "I guess I don't need to learn anything more today."

"Why is that?" Sylvia asked.

"Simple, Mommy. I learned now Emily doesn't like frogs either." He started to laugh and of course, so did Jack. The two of them were like night and day most times, but lately Jack was starting to mimic his older brother. Emily rolled her eyes again as she always did when she was disgusted or didn't know what to say. Richard looked across the table to her and went cross-eyed, teasing her.

"Now, now, Ricky, be nice to your sister or she might bop you on the nose." It was true. Emily was a feisty girl. Richard would not have been the first boy she had bopped.

"Nah, I won't bop him, Mommy. He's my stinky little brother."

"I'm not stinky, Emmy. You are." Richard stuck out his tongue, which caused his little brother to laugh almost uncontrollably.

Sylvia looked at both Richard and Emily. "Now you two stop your teasing. Come on, Emily. You'll be late for the bus if you don't hurry up."

The sun was fully out now. It shone down on the fields and valley like a beautiful halo from another world. Sylvia looked out the front room window. "It looks like we're in for a nice day. I think we can get a lot done before your father comes home. First, we will get the shopping out of the way, and then when we get back from town, we can start cleaning the hog stalls. Your father will be happy about that. He has worked so hard this past couple of weeks. I think we should take the time to start cleaning them at least to help your father out."

"Boy I'm glad I'm going to school. I helped daddy with that one time and that is a stinky job, even smellier than Richard."

"What did I say Emily?" Sylvia questioned with a stern look on her face. "Now come on, get that porridge into your belly and no more teasing."

"Yes Mom. Sorry." Emily finished her breakfast and set her bowl and empty glass in the sink. "Mommy, can you get me a pencil case today?" she asked as she trotted back into the dining room. "I don't like not having one. I lost one of my erasers yesterday."

"We'll see Emmy. I don't see why not now hurry up. The bus will be at the stop soon."

"Thanks Mom."

"Do we have to clean the hog barn?" Richard asked not looking forward to it.

"Well, we certainly won't be able to clean it all. However, it sure would be neat for your father to come home to a partly cleaned barn. Don't you think?" Sylvia was smiling. "Besides, in a few weeks your father's hired hand will be here. We hope." She was skeptical, they sent letters to prospective hired hands before, but still had not found anyone. The applicants either found other jobs or did not want to work on a hog farm.

She hoped and prayed that their new prospect, the fellow named Hudulak would be willing. She knew that the wage they offered was not exceptionally good. Nevertheless, they were also offering room and board, home cooked meals, and shower and laundry facilities. They were offering as much as any farmer who was looking for hired hands. A hog farm, however, required a lot more work than a dairy farm where the help simply put cows out to pasture, and mended the odd fence.

Hog farming was very different and time consuming. Butchering season was always the worst. They had raised only fifteen hogs the previous year, and it took Kent a long time, and a lot of hard work to butcher them. This year, they had twice as many. Only Kent knew how many he was going to have next year. Sylvia did recall him saying he wanted at least a hundred. The barn was large enough to house that many.

The amount of work that would be involved bothered her most. Kent worked hard during the week and rarely found time to do anything other than work the hogs on his days off. She wanted him to slow down a bit and to enjoy his family life. That was the main reason they were looking for a farm hand. Her concern for him finally convinced him to do so. She sipped her last bit of coffee and rose from the table as Emily came running out of her room dressed and ready for school.

Sylvia looked at her and smiled, "You look beautiful, Emmy."

"Thanks Mommy. Gotta go," Emily pulled on her fall jacket and shoes and ran out the door. Sylvia watched as her daughter headed down the road toward the bus stop. Sylvia was grinning from ear to ear. Emily was their miracle daughter as the two previous pregnancies had resulted in stillborn babies. For a brief moment, she thought back to those trying times. It had been a horribly sad time.

Now though, they had Emily and she was the apple of their eye. Emily looked back as she always did, and waved at the two faces she could see through the window. Sylvia and Richard waved back.

"Okay big boy." Sylvia looked at Richard, "we have a little while before we're going to town. You can feed the dog and check on the rabbits while I get these dishes done."

"Can Jack walk down to the barn with me and help?"

"I don't see why not. Just let me get him dressed a little warmer."

"Yay!" Richard said with enthusiasm, "I like it when he comes with me."

"I'm sure he likes being with you too. Remember to be careful. He can get hurt easily."

"Not when he's with me, he can't," Richard stated matter-of-factly. "I will always protect Jack and Emmy. Sometimes though, I don't think Emmy needs protection."

Sylvia laughed. "She's your sister Richard, and it is all right to protect her if you can, whether she wants you to or not."

Richard nodded his head. "Good 'cause I always will. Is Jack ready?"

"As soon as I get his boots on," Sylvia tied Jack's boots up. "There. He's all yours King Richard."

Richard took Jack by the hand, "We're going to go see the bunnies Jack. Are you excited?"

"Bunnies, barn," Jack said as he pointed in the direction. Young as he was, he did know a few words. *Bunnies* and *barn, yes* and *yeah* were four he knew well.

"That's right. The bunnies are down at the barn," Richard corrected him.

Jack darted ahead and Richard chased after him, the family dog nipping at their heels. Echoes of laughter, with the squawking of a few chickens broke the silence of the calm fall morning. Sylvia sat at the kitchen table as Richard and Jack did their morning chores, the coffee can with the house money in front of her. She dumped the can. Coins and paper money poured onto the table.

She did a quick count and was surprised to find that she had forty-eight dollars and sixty-two cents. She put the eight dollars and sixty-two cents back in the can and put the difference in her purse wallet. "This will do," she said to herself as she rose and put the can back in the cupboard. Noting the time to be slightly past 8:00 a.m., she poured herself a cup of tea to finish the pot off. When Richard and Jack were finished, they would leave for town. For now though, she knew the two boys would take their time. That was fine. She was not in a rush. Besides, she wanted the weather to warm up a bit before they left.

Sipping her tea, she stared out the kitchen window. Thoughts of Christmas were on her mind, even though it was not Thanksgiving yet. Christmas was the holiday she worried about mostly. It was always so hard to buy exactly what the children wanted. Although she knew they appreciated every gift they received, she always wanted to do more.

Maybe the hog harvest will bring in the extra money I want to have for the Christmas Holiday, she thought.

What she did not know was that Kent had been putting a little extra away every payday. It was to be his surprise for the whole family. He knew that they had not always had a fabulous Christmas. This year, though, he wanted it to be spectacular. There was a doll that, Emily had wanted for a long time, and the boys had wished for some Tonka Trucks and toy farm animals. This year he wanted to get those particular presents. Kent had saved $150.00 and there were still two months of saving ahead of him. He hoped to save at least double that.

Chapter 3

A few weeks after he sent the letter, Kent and his new hired hand, were to meet for the first time. It was Saturday, September 27, 1958. Hudulak was arriving by Greyhound, and Kent was meeting him at the station. He was not sure what to expect. All he knew was that this Hudulak fellow had experience as a hired hand and that he had accepted Kent and Sylvia's offer of a wage plus room and board. There was nothing out of the ordinary there.

They didn't know that Hudulak had a bit of a past. He grew up in a poor Ukrainian family and his father left home when he was young. His mother raised him as best she could. Hudulak had his problems. He had been an unusually unruly kid, always in trouble. He hated anyone with authority. He wanted to be a free bird, he would say. If he wanted something and was not able to get it the honest way, he would steal it.

He had an anger inside him that would show its ugly head every now and then, and he knew at those times that his temper was out of control. He had not hurt anyone, though, and he did not intend to. None of this information was out in the open. Kent and Sylvia knew only what he offered about himself in his letters.

The bus pulled in early on Saturday morning. Kent rose from his chair and waited patiently. A couple of men stepped out, and Kent asked if either were Alex Hudulak.

They both shook their heads, 'no'.

Finally, a dark-haired, lanky man stepped out. He was unshaved and looked tired. Kent stepped forward and asked the same question. "Hello, is your name Alex Hudulak?"

"Yes, I'm Alex. You must be Kent?" The man reached out, and the two shook hands.

"Welcome to the Kootenays," Kent said.

"Thanks."

Kent nodded and gestured with his hand for them to move on to the truck. "How was your trip?"

"Long. Why is it that a bus is always so cold," Hudulak commented as he gathered his gear.

Kent thought of that as a statement so didn't answer. They reached the truck, and Hudulak put his belongings in the back and hopped in. As soon as they were on the highway, Kent started asking questions.

"Have you worked hogs before?" he asked. In the letter, Hudulak was not clear on that. Kent wanted to make sure.

"Some, yep," Hudulak answered.

"How many hogs did you work, at one time or another?" Kent questioned.

"To be honest only a few, I mostly worked cattle, but every rancher up north also has a few hogs. I know a bit. I work hard and am a quick learner though."

"All right, just remember, when I tell you to do something I will expect you to do it. I'll show you how until you learn. After that and if I think you are worth the salt, there might be a wage increase, providing you do things my way."

Hudulak smiled at him. "You're the boss. What should I call you, boss man, Kent, or Mr. Townsend?"

"Any of them works for me, as long as it is used respectfully." The real test, he knew, would be when the man began to work.

"How far is it to home boss?" Hudulak asked as he looked around.

"Thirty miles, we'll be there in no time. Just enough time to tell you how a few things will work. For now, you will be sharing a room with my two sons. Breakfast during the week is at 5:00 a.m. Only you and I will be eating then. My wife Sylvia and the kids get up after I leave for work. She will serve you lunch at noon, or you can take a bag lunch with you. Dinner is between 5:00 pm and 6:00 pm. Weekends vary."

"That sounds okay with me. Is your wife a good cook?" Hudulak had no idea what kind of remark that was. It was a bit rude for sure, but Kent took it in stride.

"She is a great cook, but if you don't like her cooking, you don't have to eat it." He looked over to Hudulak who seemed to be staring blankly out the window. He did not even respond to Kent's reply. Kent shrugged his shoulders and shook his head.

Finally, Hudulak spoke. "Nice around here, isn't it?"

"It sure is, and where we are going is paradise," Kent said as he continued to drive. "Winters though, are a different story. Never know what it is going to be like. There are never two that are the same that's for sure."

"I've never been in these parts before. I stuck around up North and in Alberta most of my life. Only heard stories about the Kootenays, saw a few odd pictures, you know, that type of thing." Hudulak once more turned his head and stared out the window. The only sounds heard for the next while were the tires on the dirt road or pavement. Kent did not mind the silence, nor did Hudulak it seemed. Finally, he broke the silence. "I'm starting to get thirsty. Is there a place around here where I can get a drink?"

"We're almost in Fruitvale. There is a Co-op station. I'll buy you a pop."

"I was hoping for a cold beer."

"Not today. You will need to be fresh when you start working. Besides, I don't think Sylvia would appreciate me bringing home a drunken hired hand. It's pop or water, unless you want a coffee?"

"Ahh, forget it. I'll drink water once we get to your farm." Hudulak waved his hand through the air.

"Water would probably be best. It'll save me some money and a stop," Kent mentioned as they continued. He did not want to sound angry, but Hudulak was already making his patience wear thin. Asking for beer before he even arrived at the job made him wonder how he was going to turn out after all. He blamed it on the long trip Hudulak travelled that day. The man was probably hungry and tired. Kent accepted that as the reason for his ignorance. The drive continued in silence until they turned down Hudu Road.

"Are we getting close now?" Hudulak asked, with a grim smile.

"Just down the road a ways," Kent replied.

It was still early morning and dew in the fields glistened like diamonds. They saw a deer as it bounced across the dirt road and dashed into a neighboring field.

"That was a big fellow wasn't it?" Hudulak watched the deer as it pranced away.

Kent looked over to Hudulak who was pretending to hold a rifle and shoot the deer.

"BAM!" he shouted. "Got 'em in the head, boss man," he said as he began to chuckle. "Do you hunt, boss man?"

"I have occasionally, but I prefer to leave the wild animals alone. That is why I raise hogs and chickens. Hope to raise a few head of cattle eventually."

"There isn't anything like a big beef steak. Venison is pretty good too though."

"So you are a hunter?" Kent asked.

"I've hunted a bit. Not in the last few years though. I've been too busy working. Ahh, well, you know how that goes. Work, work, work, men have to make a living."

"They sure do," Kent was beginning to relax. It sounded as though Hudulak liked to work hard. That was always a good sign. His attitude however he could do without he seemed a little odd. Other than that, maybe there was a hard worker beneath it all. "A hard working man is a man worth his wage," Kent said as a matter-of-factly, not to imply anything, rather that was his belief. Hard work never hurt anyone. It built character.

"I like it when my hands blister, and the skin peels away. Hurts a bit, but hard work and pain go hand in hand,"

Hudulak was looking at the palms of his hands in an odd way.

Kent turned his head and focused on the road. "There are always gloves," he made a point to say.

"Nah, who needs them," Hudulak said as he turned his head.

They were quiet for a few minutes until Kent spoke up. "There she is. There is our home," he pointed to a white house at the foot of a hill. "You can see the barn from here too. We have a garden next to the house. Sylvia and my daughter Emily look after that. Both have green thumbs. I'm good at raising hogs; I leave the vegetables to them."

Hudulak looked on. "That is a real attractive place, boss man. I bet your wife takes good care of the house. Cleaning it and keeping it cozy all the time. Women are good at that. They look real cute too when they're doing it."

There was no call for Hudulak to have said that, and Kent looked at him. "I'd ask that you don't talk like that around my wife and daughter, or you might find yourself walking down this dirt road."

"I meant no harm, boss man. I'll watch my P's and Q's when I'm in their presence, don't worry."

Kent nodded at him. "Good." They pulled up to the house, and stepped out of the truck.

Hudulak stretched his back and cracked his neck. "Ah, that feels better. I get so cramped and stiff if I don't stand occasionally. I hate long drives, and that bus ride was long." He grabbed his gear from the back of the truck, and Kent gestured for him to follow.

Opening the front door to the house, Kent called out, "We're here Sylvia."

She met them at the door and kissed Kent on the cheek. "Hello. You must be Alex Hudulak?" she reached out to shake his hand.

"Yes ma'am. Most call me Hudulak, but you can call me Alex if you like." He was smitten with her at first sight, and before the handshake ended, he had a hundred thoughts about her. *None were good.*

Chapter 4

With the introduction over, the three moved into the dining room and sat down to some fresh coffee.

"Do you take cream and sugar Alex?" Sylvia asked.

"Yes ma'am, thanks," he was looking directly at her, his stomach filled with butterflies. He hated when that happened, and it always seemed to happen in the presence of women. He was not a handsome man, average in his mind. That is why he always resorted to getting his women drunk first. It was the only way he knew how to get *lucky*.

That is what, he was thinking now, if he could get her drunk and be alone with her he would not waste any time making advances toward her and ripping off her clothes. He averted his eyes and looked across the fields.

"I think you folks have a nice place here, I haven't seen many places like this. Most of the farms I worked on were ragged and run down, not this here though, no sir. The inside here too is fine. You must spend hours a day keeping it clean."

It was a statement with a hidden agenda. Hudulak had already been fantasizing about her. He imagined her bending over dusting, mopping floors and doing laundry. It was a sick fantasy that he always thought about, spying on a woman while she cleaned. Brought back to the here and now as Sylvia set the coffee pot on the table, his *sick fantasy* faded into the back of his *sick mind*.

"Yes, with three little ones running around it does get hectic. That is why I am so glad Kent hired you. Now I can spend more time with the kids, won't have to feed the hogs anymore." She looked over to Kent who was pouring a cup of coffee, a smile on her face. "Isn't that right Kent?"

"Well, he's been hired to work the hogs, not the rabbits. Someone will have to keep them fed and watered. I don't think you are out of the woods yet, honey," he smiled back at her. "But once we get fixed on what is what and who is who, I don't think you'll be needed down at the barn anymore."

He was looking at Sylvia as he said that, and he could see the relief on her face. He knew how much work she had to handle, with running the house, keeping the kids happy and, of course, dealing with the farm chores while he was at work. He was glad all that was going to change. She would be able to spend more time with the kids and her household duties. The farm chores were the hard work, in his opinion. He had no idea the housekeeping was also a lot of hard, tedious work. Sylvia was happy running the house. It was something she knew how to do well, although she was not praised for the work, she knew how much Kent and the kids appreciated it. For her, that was good enough.

"You got rabbits too?" Hudulak asked.

"About fifteen, they're to keep the kids busy. I harvest a dozen or so a year and sell them to the Italians. Have you ever eaten rabbit?"

"No sir. Not farm raised ones. I shot a couple wild ones though. I cooked them on a skewer over a fire. It was during one of the cattle drives I helped with I hated doing that, you know, cattle roundups. I am not too keen on horses and they don't seem to like me much either. I wouldn't mind so much if it didn't involve riding a horse," Hudulak, mentioned as a means of conversing.

"Every farm or ranch ought to have a couple of horses I think. We'll be getting a couple. That way the kids can learn to ride them. You won't have to worry about using them to roundup cattle. I won't be getting any cattle anytime soon. I may in a few years, but right now, I want to concentrate on raising hogs. I'll leave the beef to the other farmers. Might get a dairy cow, but not for a while." Kent brought his coffee cup to his lips and took a sip.

"How many hogs are we going to be butchering this season?" Hudulak wanted to know.

"Thirty. Next year we'll be harvesting a hundred or so."

27

"Ahh, thirty isn't going to take too long to butcher when the time comes. What, two days?"

"I've only got the weekend off so two days it is. The butchering season is fast approaching too."

"A couple more weeks at least though, right?"

"Probably, yep," Kent nodded, "Once we finish with our coffee, we'll take a walk down to the hog barn, and I'll show you around."

"Sure. Is there much work to do today?"

"Not until this evening's chores. You will be welcome to help me then. Your paid work though won't start until Monday."

"That sounds good. Is it all right if I take a nap later?"

"You could do that, sure," Kent said.

"Can you show me where?"

"Like I said earlier, you are in with the boys, but they are still asleep, after I show you around they'll be awake. Then you can stow your gear and have a bit of a nap yourself if you like."

"How old are the boys?"

"Richard is five, and Jack is two. Our daughter Emmy is eight. She will be nine soon. Right now, she is visiting up the road with a neighbor girl. You'll meet them all later."

Hudulak nodded as he took the last swig from his coffee. "I can't wait. Well, my coffee is finished, boss man." Hudulak set his cup down, "I'm ready for the grand tour."

"All right then. Let's go." Kent rose from the table, and Hudulak followed.

"Should I slip on my boots or will my walking shoes do?"

"It's a hog barn. Use your own judgment," Kent said as he slipped on his gumboots. Stepping through the door, he stood on the small porch, pulled out his pipe, and filled it with tobacco as he waited. Drawing a flame over it, he inhaled the pungent tobacco smoke. He looked up the road and towards the forest. The trees were beginning to change color. He listened to the sounds of the valley. A dog barked, and he could hear the echo in the distance. A light breeze gently blew the smoke from his pipe. He inhaled another lung-full then tapped the remaining tobacco out onto the ground. He stepped on the embers with his heel and tucked the pipe back into his work jacket pocket. He leaned on the hood of his truck and waited some more.

Finally, Hudulak stepped out wearing his boots. *I guess he isn't that daft after all,* Kent thought as he met Hudulak at the bottom of the stairs. "Should get a pair of pull-on rubber boots like mine," he said as he pointed at his own boots.

"Can't wear the rubber boots, they make my feet sweat, then I end up with blisters and such. Nope, I'll stick with the leather tie-ups. They got the steel toe too, so they're good for kicking things," Hudulak half chuckled, as they turned and walked toward the barn. "Yep, boss man, I'd say you have a real nice spread here. How many acres do you have forty, or fifty?"

"Seventy-five acres actually, a lot of it is on the mountainside. What you can see is maybe half of what we own. I can't do much with the land on the mountain though. Rocky as can be. Nothing grows there except mountain ash and stinging nettle. I guess I will graze cattle up that way if I get any. I'll keep it as it is for now. Maybe the kids will use it when they grow up."

The two began walking toward the hog barn, and Kent pointed things out. "Hudu Creek is over there at the edge of the field. The neighbor kids fish there. A better spot is Beaver Creek where we crossed that long bridge. The first barn you see is the rabbit and hay barn. The other is where I house the hogs." Kent unlatched the main barnyard gate and swung it open. "We like to keep the gate closed, so, make sure you latch it back up every time."

Continuing to the hay barn, Kent showed Hudulak where to find the hog feed and fresh straw that he used to lay in the hog stalls. The barn had been built years before he bought the farm it was old and weathered, and would cost a fortune someday to fix the roof when it needed to be redone, but it was perfect for what he needed right now. It was immense, with the bottom half closed in and the loft part wide open with openings for windows on one side. It was perfect for storing the hay and housing the small animals. There were rooms in the lower part for the chickens and rabbits.

"The rabbits are through that door there," he said as he pointed at the door. "The water we use for the hogs and rabbits is outside on the side of the hog barn. I plumbed that in when we first moved here. In recent years, it froze up in the winter. If that happens, you can carry it from the house or the creek. Either way, it is a pain in the ass and takes a bit of doing."

"Trekking through the snow must be a real pain. I bet you don't get less than four or five feet a winter eh?"

"About that, yep, the neighbor ploughs a trail for us if we need to use the creek. It hasn't frozen over in a couple of years so she probably won't freeze this winter either. I also insulated the pipes better this past summer. I think we'll be all right."

"It wouldn't matter to me any. Work is work, whether hauling it from the house or the creek. If that's what needs to be done, then that is what we do, right boss man?"

"Let's hope you have that same attitude in three or four months when the winter is at it's coldest."

"I've been in cold weather before, boss man, it doesn't bother me. You just keep moving and work hard. That is all you have to do to warm up."

"True enough," Kent agreed. Finally arriving at the hog barn and thirty squealing hogs, he opened the sturdy wooden door. The smell of wet straw and hog feed wafted towards them, followed by the discernible smell of hog waste. He built the barn with his own blood, sweat, and tears. It was one of a kind or so Kent thought. He built it with pigs in mind, but if he chose, it could house other animals too.

It was long, with a huge room at one end, which housed a boiler. The boiler heated the water they needed when they harvested hogs and used to keep the hogs warm in cold weather. The barn had eight stalls on either side of a wide cement walkway. Each stall had a door that latched and a feeding area. At the other end of the corridor was a double door to let the animals in and out. It was the perfect set up.

"Whew, now that stinks," Hudulak, commented as they stepped in.

"Wait until we get to clean the stalls. You'll certainly smell it then."

"I can imagine," Hudulak said as he followed Kent down the barn corridor to the sixteen stalls, five of which had a half a dozen hogs in each. "Those are neat looking hogs. Nice and fat, going to get some good chops I bet from them."

"I switched them over to a high fiber feed. That seems to fatten them up a little more than straight hog feed. We also give them all our garden waste. I'm a little concerned about that one over there though." Kent pointed at a runt. "I don't think he'll be worth much. We'll probably stuff him into our own freezer."

"You don't suppose he is sick do you?"

"Nope, they've all been checked by the vet. He's a wiener hog, I think." Kent looked over to Hudulak and smiled.

"A wiener hog? I haven't heard that before."

"That is what I call the hogs that are smaller than the others. Not sure that is the proper term, but it's what I use."

"Yeah, he probably won't gain much more weight before butchering season," Hudulak stated.

"Maybe another few pounds, but I'm not counting on it," said Kent as they proceeded down the corridor to another stall, "these fellows here though, they have some weight to them. These are the biggest of the thirty we have. Some of them are over two hundred pounds easily. That should be the average weight of all of them, two hundred and twenty-five to two hundred and fifty pounds. These are above average.

31

They are the first bunch I started on that high fiber hog feed I mentioned earlier. They have had a bit of a head start on the others. Next year I will start them all at the same time with the same high fiber food, and I hope that they will all reach the two hundred and fifty mark. That is my goal anyway."

"Isn't there a breed of hog that gets big?" Hudulak asked with interest.

"Oh they'd get fat all right if I kept them for another year, but then they'd have more fat than meat. It is best to keep them at or near the two hundred and fifty pound mark. That, by the way is hot weight, or if you like live weight. Butchered and gutted they weigh less. When you keep them at that weight, you tend to get better hams and roasts, not to mention a finer pork chop too. From these thirty, I hope to get around six thousand pounds of saleable product. However, it never turns out that way, and usually it is off by a couple hundred pounds each time I make a guess. Only time will tell I suppose."

"So what you are saying is that, by the time these fellows make it to the butcher, they might weigh out at about one hundred or so pounds a side, with their guts gone and all."

"Around that, it is an average figure. They could weigh more than we expect. The fellow who sells me the piglets has a sow he has had for as long as I have been dealing with him, that weighs almost a thousand pounds. It is a mother sow, and that is why she weighs so much. His breeding boar is probably as heavy."

"Wow. A thousand-pound sow, now that is big. How does something that huge even get bred?"

Kent got a chuckle from that himself, but refrained from answering the question to keep Hudulak from asking other irrelevant questions.

"It doesn't matter to me, I only buy the piglets. Anyway, should we head back to the house? Or do you have any other questions?"

"Nah, I'm pretty content with what we talked about so far. Maybe after this evening's chores I'll have a question or two. Right now though, to tell you the truth boss man, I'm pretty tired."

"All right then, let's head back to the house. The kids will probably be awake by now, and you can get settled."

"That sounds good to me. See you all later, hogs," Hudulak said as they made their way down the long corridor.

"That is a pretty big barn boiler eh," he mentioned as he stopped to look at it for a moment.

"How many chunks of wood or coal can you slam into that? I haven't seen many that large."

"When I use it, I toss in about six three-foot logs, all at about four to six inches in diameter. I have used coal in it too, and I usually throw in half a wheelbarrow full. The coal burns all night. I prefer using wood as the smoke from wood is easier to breathe when the wind blows it to the house."

"I guess the water tank on top of the boiler is near a hundred gallons or so?"

"Probably close to. When we butcher, we keep it full of hot water at all times."

"Does it heat up the water quickly?" Hudulak asked.

Kent was somewhat impressed with Hudulak's knowledge of such a boiler.

"You know a little bit about these types of boilers I suspect."

"Yes. I worked for a chicken processor in Alberta a few years back, and the process of heating up the water used before they go through the feather-plucker was the same. Except, I think they used coal all the time. A couple of others and I had to reline the inside with brick, and high heat mortar once. It was all sticky and corroded from the coal. It took me a week to have the tar washed off. I hated that job. I would never want to do it again that is for sure."

"Well, this one also heats up the barn during the winter. I have a neighbor who brings me a dozen cords of wood a year. It keeps the hogs happy and prevents them from getting pneumonia or other lung ailments from being cold. I can't afford to lose any, you know. That is another reason we toss down straw too. It keeps them off the cold concrete floors."

"Do you have an outside pen for them?"

"We have a small one. We put them out in sets of ten during the day, but we bring them in at night. Each day another set goes out. I have considered building a bigger pen. There are coyotes and dogs running around. I've never left any hogs outside overnight. I wouldn't want to lose any."

"True enough," Hudulak replied as they made their way to the barn door. The sun was warming things up, and it beat down on their faces as they walked to the house.

"It'll be a warm day I think. The sun sure feels good doesn't it, boss man?"

"Yeah, but I'm afraid winter is knocking on our door."

Chapter 5

The days came and went. Hudulak proved himself a quick learner hard worker. One of his quirks that Kent noticed right from the start was the way he would burst out in a rage if things were not going his way. He would calm down after a few moments, and continue with his work. Kent and Sylvia learned to accept that behavior.

It seemed as time went by Hudulak was in his element. The butchering was a success. Hudulak worked his hardest, with some glee. Kent thought it a bit strange how he seemed to enjoy the hog slaughter. The blood in his hair, on his hands, and on his face did not bother him at all. Kent, on the other hand always washed off the blood whenever he had the chance.

"You are going to need to wash up before you come in the house. We'll get a tub of warm water for you to use."

"Sure thing boss man, it doesn't bother me right now. I'll wash off what I can when we're done. There isn't many more to go now. Am getting a bit hungry though, isn't it lunch time yet?"

"Not yet. Another hour to go or there about, I'm having some sandwiches and a thermos brought to us. No use dirtying up the house with our stench until the end of the day," Kent chuckled.

Hudulak was standing there as though he was in deep thought. Then, like a flick of a switch he said, "Well, best get back to it then. I was down here to get some rifle shells. Where do you keep them, boss man?"

"Right there on the shelf by the door," Kent pointed. "They've always been there."

"Oh yeah, that's right. Thanks, boss man." Hudulak turned to retrieve a handful of the small caliber bullets, taking notice that there was also a box of .22 Long bullets. Kent told him to use only the .22 Short. Instead, he reached for the .22 Long bullets and stuffed his pockets. He didn't understand Kent's reasoning. In fact, he doubted Kent had one. Besides, he wanted to see if there would be more damage done to the hog with the .22 Long Rifle bullets, as opposed to the Shorts he had been using. The .22 Long Rifle bullets were for coyotes, stray dogs, or anything that tried to cause harm to Kent's livestock. Hudulak was about to discover the reason why Kent suggested using the smaller bullet.

With his shirt pocket full, he made his way to the fourth hog pen that housed five hogs. The squealing hogs ran around his feet, and he kicked at them.

"Get out of here you hog bastards," he said as he cornered one of the bigger hogs, and loaded the rifle. Taking aim, he slowly pulled the trigger. The loud *BANG* echoed, and the bullet passed through the hog, ricocheted off the concrete floor and whizzed into the wall on the other side.

Kent came running down the barn corridor.

"What the hell was that!" he exclaimed, with both anger and fear that something may have happened to his hired help.

"Oh Geez, boss man, I must of grabbed the wrong bullets. Man was that ever stupid of me. Killed the hog well though, knocked him down like a sledge hammer nailing a rail road spike."

"Never mind that, you'd better be more careful next time," Kent stated with authority.

"Uhuh, sure will boss man." Hudulak was nodding his head in agreement, but deep down he had been amused. It all happened so quickly. He grabbed the pig-sticking knife from the sheath on his belt, and with half a smile stuck it deep into the hog's throat pulling the blade out only when warm blood spurted from the hole. He liked that part of the slaughter, the gutting and cleaning he left to Kent.

It was a straightforward process. He slaughtered them, and Kent dressed them. The real work of the farm was not harvesting the hogs, but in carefully raising them. That was something Hudulak had yet to experience, but his time was coming. Kent intended to increase the number of hogs he raised and with that came a lot of extra work. He hoped Hudulak could handle it, but he was not sure. His selection in hiring Hudulak was partly due to his delay in hiring someone else. For now, he would certainly give his hired hand the benefit of the doubt.

He had worked hard from the first day and Kent appreciated that. Hudulak could have turned out to be lazy and ineffective. So far, he had done well. He did have his moments, though, and the accident with the wrong bullets was one of them. Kent shook his head as he pulled the next hog on the line over to the forty five-gallon drum of boiling water that he used to loosen the hog's bristle-like hair.

Dipping the hog carcass a few times and satisfied it was ready, he moved over to the table where he scraped all the hair away. Then he lifted it up on the pulley again and over to the wheelbarrow that he used to hold the hogs' innards. He cut open the stomach, and shoved his hands deep inside. He gave a good pull, and the guts tore out with a ripping sound and fell into the wheelbarrow. He moved the hog carcass next to the other seven he needed to cut in half. Continuing, he called for Hudulak's help.

"Hey Alex, come here and give me a hand for a minute," Kent hollered down the barn corridor. He wanted Hudulak not so much to help but to start training him with the procedures. Hudulak needed to know this part of the work. Kent wanted anyone working for him to be able to handle both sides of the butchering process.

"We got four more on the way, boss man," Hudulak said as he stood next to Kent. "What do you want me to do?"

"Grab that rope," Kent was pointing at the one that had another carcass on it. "Pull it over that barrel with the boiling water and lower it in a couple of times."

"Sure thing, is that water going to soften the hog's hide?"

It was an intelligent question for a change, and Kent was a bit surprised. "That is exactly what it does. That way we can scrape the hairs off. Otherwise, you would be scraping for a month of Sundays. And no one wants to work on a Sunday," he said with humor.

Hudulak chuckled, "That's a good one, boss man. I wouldn't want to work on a Sunday unless I had to, like now because of the hogs," he dipped the hog in the hot water. "Man that sure doesn't smell too nice... Whew. I'll dunk it one more time for good measure. There, now I guess I pull it along to here," he pointed at the table with all the hair stuck to it, "now we scrape away. Right boss man?"

"That is right, now get it on over here, we don't want it to cool down too much." Kent walked around the table and grabbed the rope. They gave it a good tug, and it swung around. "Hold it there," Kent said as he positioned himself better. "Okay, let her down slowly. Once it is down, grab a scraper and pull it towards you in a half circle motion over the hog's hide. The hair should fall out with a bit of elbow grease."

"I'm ready boss man, let's get to it," Hudulak said. They dunked the hog a couple of times because he wasn't as quick as Kent would have liked him to be, but he did show promise. Thirty minutes later, after he took pleasure in gutting the hog it hung with the others, he had done a better job with that, Kent noted then scraping the hair away. He was indeed a strange one.

However, since he worked hard and got along with the Townsend children, Kent and Sylvia ignored his quirkiness. Emily though knew there was something about him that made her feel uneasy and sometimes scared when she was around him. He always had a look in his eyes that made her skin crawl, especially after she had taken her evening bath. It was always the same look, blank and scary and always made her get goose bumps. However, since her mom and dad seemed to like Hudulak and often discussed how hard he worked, she didn't mention her concerns and instead learned to ignore his stares.

It was a different story for Richard and Jack. To them, Hudulak seemed like the fun uncle that one sees only on holidays. He wrestled with them and took them fishing down to the creek. He didn't mind pulling Jack in the wagon so Jack could be part of the adventure. The two Townsend boys thought Hudulak was the coolest thing since canned sandwich meat, however Emily saw another part of him that no one else saw. For her, Hudulak was what nightmares were made from.

By day's end, both Kent and Hudulak were exhausted. They managed to butcher fifteen hogs that day. Another fifteen remained. They would finish the job the following day. For now, all they wanted was to clean themselves and their mess up. Tired and hungry, they made their way back to the house.

"That was a good day, boss man. I'm a bit tired, but I know I earned my wage."

"Indeed you did. Another hard day's work and we will be done, and the hogs will be on their way to the butcher shop. I am sure Dacker's Meat Packing will give us a decent price for them. They weighed in nicely this time around."

"Yeah, a few were pretty fat. The rest were probably average, eh?"

"A little better than average, I would say."

Kent took his pipe out of his coverall pocket and filled it with pipe tobacco. Bringing it to his lip's he struck a match and inhaled the acrid smoke deeply.

"Yep, it was a good day. Tomorrow will be better, when we finish. Then we don't have to worry about it again until next fall."

"Ah, it wasn't so bad," Hudulak, responded as they made their way through the gate.

At the house, they could smell food cooking.

"Sure smells good. What do you think Sylvia is cooking for us, boss man? I'm guessing roast chicken. That is what it smells like to me."

39

"You are probably right, smells like that to me too." Kent opened the front door, and they stepped inside. "Yep, that is chicken alright," Kent smiled.

"I knew it was," Hudulak replied as he removed his boots. "Hope it isn't ready yet though, I'd like to have a hot shower."

"Well, you go ahead. Don't use all the hot water. I'll need a shower too." Kent removed his own boots and coveralls, and then made his way to the dining room table and a cup of hot coffee.

"How did the butchering go?" Sylvia asked as he made himself comfortable.

"As good as I would have thought. Got fifteen done." Kent took a sip of his coffee.

"I will give Hudulak this. He's a hard worker. He is a little bit slow at a couple of things, but he works hard and tries to do his best. I think we did okay in hiring him."

"That is good to hear. He has worked hard since the first day. I am not too fond of some of his mannerisms, but I don't think he means any harm. I'm glad he is working out."

"Yep, me too," Kent replied as he filled his pipe for the second time.

As Hudulak made his way through the living room and towards the bathroom for a shower, he noticed the kids lying on the floor and coloring.

"How are you guys today?" he asked as he searched for a towel in the linen closet.

"Fine," they said in unison.

"Are you and dad finished with the butchering?" Richard asked.

"Nope, not yet," Hudulak replied as he tucked a towel under his arm.

"Can I help?" Richard asked, with enthusiasm.

"I doubt your dad would let you this year. But, eat all your veggies and maybe next year he'll let you."

"Really! Do you think so?"

"You would have to ask him, I think. I can't say either way." Hudulak stepped into the bathroom and closed the door.

"Did you hear that? Maybe next year I could help dad and Alex."

"Yuk. If that is what you want to do Richard," Emily said in her, 'that is gross' voice.

"You are jealous."

"Jealous of what, that you might be able to help next year? I doubt that Richard. I would never want to help with that messy job."

"Ah, you are just a girl anyways," Richard said as he went back to his coloring book.

Rising from the table, Kent took his cup of coffee and walked into the living room.

"Hello kids, how was your day?" he asked as he sat down in his favorite chair.

"It was okay. I helped mom with peeling the potatoes, and she even let me wash the chicken," Emily said.

"Yeah, and she didn't want to at first. She didn't like touching it," Richard reported.

"That is not true. I did what mom asked."

"Sure you did," Richard rolled his eyes and went back to coloring.

"Sounds like the three of you have been busy. Good. I am glad you helped your mom Emily. You have to learn things like that sooner or later."

"I guess so," she replied, as though she actually did not want to learn that stuff yet.

"Just like I have to learn how to help you and Alex with the butchering, right Dad?"

"You'll get your chance with that soon enough. Besides, you already help by bringing us our lunch. For now, that is good."

"But I want to learn how to butcher. Alex said if I eat my veggies maybe I could help next year, could I, Dad?

"Next year, huh, we'll see how it goes." Kent took a swig of coffee and then put the cup down on the coffee table.

"Are you going to play the harmonica tonight?" Emily asked.

"I might. Would you like it if I did?"

"Yes. We haven't done that in a while."

"No, you are right, we haven't. If we don't do it tonight, I promise we will do it tomorrow night for sure. How is that?"

"I suppose," Emily said as she sat next to him.

"Yuk, Daddy. You have some slime in your hair... Gross." Emily stood up quickly and moved to the couch.

"What is the matter Emmy? Are you afraid of a little pig guts?" Richard teased as he stood up to look at it.

"She's right Dad, you got some pig guts in your hair."

"I'll get rid of it before we eat. Don't worry it isn't going to hurt you." Kent chuckled as he took a long puff from his pipe before tapping it out into the ashtray. "Good thing I wore coveralls or I wouldn't be as clean as I am now."

Sylvia hearing the conversation stood in the doorway of the living room looking on. "You are far from clean Kent. How long has Alex been in the bathroom?" she asked, with her hands on her hips. "Dinner is going to be ready in a few more minutes. Better tell him to get a move on so you can wash up too."

"He'll be done shortly. I am not worried about it," Kent replied.

"All right, then I'll tell him to get a move on." Sylvia made her way to the bathroom door and knocked. "Alex hurry up, Kent needs to wash up too. Dinner is going to be ready shortly. Hurry up now."

"I'll be finished in a second, boss lady," Hudulak responded from the other side of the door. Shutting off the water, he stepped out and looked at himself in the mirror. *Ah, I'll shave later. Wouldn't want the boss lady getting too bossy,* he thought as he dried off. *Damn woman anyway.*

He never like women and most didn't like him. They found him to be unkempt, loathsome, and dirty. In his mind, women were good for one thing only, sexual gratification that was all. Sylvia though was different. He thought for sure that she was attracted to him in a not so casual way. He sat up many times at night and fantasized about her and Emily. As far as he knew, no one suspected this about him. He was wrong though.

Emily had her suspicions. There was more to Hudulak than his being an ordinary hired hand. She was not blind to the fact that he looked at both her and her mom in a way that was worrisome there was nothing she could say though after all, she was just a kid.

The bathroom door opened, and Hudulak stepped out. "The shower is free now, boss man. She's all yours." Stepping into the bedroom he shared with Richard and Jack, he tossed his dirty clothes on the floor at the foot of his bed. He made his way to the kitchen, poured himself a cup of coffee, and sat down at the table. "We put in a good days work today boss lady. Supper sure smells good," he took a drink of coffee and waited for Sylvia responded.

"Yes, you guys did," she reached into the oven to remove the chicken. Setting it on the counter to cool, she drained the potatoes and mixed vegetables.

"Do you need a hand with anything?" he asked.

He was there because he wanted to watch her as she finished preparing their dinner. He liked how she looked and knew there was nothing he could help with.

"No, not really, Alex," Sylvia responded not noticing how he was looking at her.

"Oh, okay. Well, it sure looks and smells good," he commented as he returned to the table.

"Thanks. I hope you worked up an appetite."

"I did," he responded. *In many ways,* he thought as he peeked around the corner from where he sat and watched her.

"Good because I made plenty. You guys will eat chicken salad sandwiches for a week," Sylvia joked.

"That is okay. I like chicken salad."

Hudulak took another swig of his coffee.

"You made some pretty good coffee too."

"Nope, Emily made that."

"Really, wow. Hey Emmy, you made some good coffee," he said, hoping she would come to the table so he could look at her too.

Emily heard him, but she was not about to go to the dining room and be alone with him. She simply responded politely. "Thanks Alex, I'm glad you like it. I've only made it a few times."

"Maybe you should make the coffee all the time."

"What, you don't like my coffee?" Sylvia piped up from the kitchen, teasing of course.

"I sure do. I like anything you make, boss lady."

"Good answer," Sylvia joked.

Chapter 6

Rising bright and early the following morning, after a quick coffee and a couple of boiled eggs, the two men headed out to finish the hog harvest. The sun was shining in a most spectacular way. The ground glistened as crystal-clear droplets of thawing frost formed on the blades of browning grass. The two men inhaled deeply.

"Nice day out. Hope it stays like this. Nothing like the sunrise to get a man pumped, eh, boss man?"

"That and a good strong cup of coffee," Kent replied, with good spirits.

"It's a shame the day is going to be a messy one."

"Ah, that is okay. We'll have the sun," Hudulak was smiling as he and Kent walked the distance to the hog barn.

"Geez, hold on a second," he stopped and stood still.

Kent was next to him and turned.

"What's the matter?" he asked, with general concern.

"Oh, it was nothing. I used to be an epileptic. It is under control now. Every once in a while I get a bit dizzy."

"What do you mean used to be?" Kent wanted to know.

"When I was younger, the doctors put me on medication. By the time, I was in my teens I didn't have to take it anymore because the seizures stopped. I read in a medical magazine that epilepsy sometimes comes and goes. I haven't had a problem with it in years and years. I'm cured. Although once in a while, I sometimes get dizzy. Not sure, it has anything to do with epilepsy. Usually a couple of aspirin takes care of it. I'm okay now though. Come on, boss man. Let's get to butchering hogs," Hudulak said with glee.

They continued their brisk walk to the hog barn. Although only coals remained in the boiler, it was warm inside.

"Nice in here isn't it?" Hudulak grabbed an arm full of wood. "It'll be even nicer once the boiler heats up more. It shouldn't take longer than an hour at most."

"About that, yep," Kent responded. "While it is heating up we'll get the water going and have a go at sharpening the butchering knives. The sharper they are, the better the job."

"I wouldn't disagree with that."

Opening the boiler door Hudulak tossed in the pieces of wood. They caught fire instantly, and began to crackle and snap. He held his hands close as he warmed them up a bit. Closing the boiler door, he stood and walked over to the makeshift bench Kent had put together with a couple of planks and sawhorses so he could sharpen the knives. Hudulak watched in amazement.

"You are sure good at sharpening."

"I've had a lot of practice over the years. Want to give it a try?"

"Nah, I'd probably cut off a finger."

"Not if you do it right."

"I'll let you do it this time around, boss man. I'll watch. Maybe I'll learn."

"We don't have time for you to be standing around. Get the tank on top of the boiler full of water. The water has to get good and hot. Otherwise, we'll be scraping the hides forever and a day."

"Good point, boss man. I'll get to it."

He walked to the water hose and turned it on. After taking a drink, he stuck the hose into the top of the water tank and waited as it filled. He stood and stared blankly into the top of the tank. Kent noticed this and stroked his chin.

"You all right, Alex?"

"Um, yeah, sure, I'm okay. Why do you ask?"

"I thought there might have been a problem."

"I was watching the water swirl around is all it sure is slow in filling this tank, today."

"It has the same water pressure as the house. It might take a few minutes to fill."

"It seems like it has already been forever. Was it this slow yesterday?"

"Think about that for a minute. If it is the same as it was yesterday, then I guess it's going to take the same amount of time," Kent turned back to sharpening the knives and rolled his eyes.

"You know what, boss man. Maybe I didn't turn it on all the way," Hudulak, said with some confusion.

"Maybe you should double check," Kent suggested.

Hudulak turned and walked the short distance to where the tap was and sure enough realized he hadn't turned it on all the way, "That was the problem boss man," he shook his head. "I think my head is lighter than air this morning."

"Ah, a simple mistake is all that was," he didn't want Hudulak to feel too incompetent. "Check the fill rate now."

"Oh yeah, she's coming through good now. How is the knife sharpening coming, boss man?" He looked up and across the floor where Kent was standing.

"A couple more to go, they'll be extremely sharp, so be careful when you use them."

"I only need the pig-sticking knife boss." Hudulak looked back into the tank of swirling water. "We should be butchering the hogs around 9:00 o'clock I suppose."

Kent nodded, "That's when the water will probably be hot enough. Bring in some more wood and get that boiler blazing. The two stalls that are empty from yesterday's butchering should be cleaned, by the time we get all that done, the water will be ready."

"That is a good idea, keeps us busy."

"A man can't make money if he doesn't work," Kent said, with a chuckle.

"Yeah, you got that right. Say, how long have I worked here? A couple of months I think, isn't it?"

"You started in September, a little over a month. Is there a problem?"

"No, no. Nothing, like that, I was wondering if you and Sylvia dip into the sauce once in a while."

"You mean drink?"

"Yeah, you know, have a beer or a shot of rum."

"We do on occasion. We have friends, the Smith's, that stop by every now and again. We play cards, and old man Smith usually brings a case of beer. The women might have one, but they prefer wine."

"I was wondering because I haven't had a cold beer in a long time, wouldn't mind one once in a while. Would it bother you, boss man, if I had Sylvia pick me up a case the next time she's in town? I'll pay for it from my wage, of course."

"There will be no drinking on the job. You can feel free to drink on your own time. Just don't make it a habit. I have no problem with a man that has an odd drink, but I would not put up with a man working for me who drank every chance he had. Does that answer your question?"

"It sure does, you wouldn't have to worry about me drinking often. I always feel like I have the flu bug the next day. An occasional cold beer would sure be nice."

"For a cool drink, I prefer iced tea or juice; sometimes I don't mind a pop."

"To each their own like they say, I guess," Hudulak shrugged.

"I suppose I would agree with that," Kent said as he finished sharpening the last knife. "Knives are done. I'll finish up with the water, and you can start by filling up the boiler with wood."

"Yep," Hudulak stepped down from the platform that he stood on while filling the tank. "She's full now."

"Good, good," Kent responded as Hudulak made his way outside to the woodpile.

Loading up with an arm-full of wood he made his way back inside. "Sheesh, the sun's gone now. It's turning grey and cloudy," he said as he set the wood down and opened the boiler door. Tossing the wood inside, he warmed his hands. "So, I'm betting we're in for a storm today. Strange how the weather changed."

"It is fall after all. A little rain isn't going to hurt us one bit."

"Heck no, just makes things a little sloppy is all," Hudulak smiled.

"Well, it'll be fitting for how messy we're going to get."

"True enough," Hudulak nodded as he grabbed the gutter shovel. "I'm going to get started on cleaning those stalls. Are we going to lay out new straw?"

"No point in doing that. Not going to have any livestock to bed down in them once these hogs are gone, not for a while anyway."

"Good enough," Hudulak responded. "When are you going to get the new piglets?"

"Sometimes I get them in late fall-early winter. It depends. If we get decent prices on these, I'll probably pick up next year's pigs before Christmas."

"That's a few months away."

"Yep, no worries, though. We will have plenty of work until then. Mostly fixing the barns and doing some landscaping. We need to work on fences before the ground freezes. You'll be busy."

"Good to know. I don't like sitting idle for too long."

"If I didn't have enough work to keep you busy after the butchering I wouldn't have been looking for help," Kent assured.

As Hudulak made his way down the long corridor to the first stall, Sylvia came in. Kent turned and looked. "Hey, morning sweetheart, what brings you down here?"

"Brought you guy's some hot coffee. It's getting chilly out, thought you might like some." Sylvia made her way over to where Kent was filling the last drum with water.

"Thank you. Set it down by the knives. It's the only table out here," he was smiling at her as he said that.

"I was going to bring you some fresh buns too, but they haven't risen yet. They'll be ready for lunch, though. Would you guys like soup or stew, today?"

"Ah, either or. It doesn't matter to me. As long as it's hot. Fresh bread sounds good."

"I have a pie to bake too, but that will be for supper."

"Pie?" Kent asked.

"Yes. It is Sunday after all. You know I like to bake on Sundays. Oh yeah, I was supposed to give you a hug from Emily and Richard. So, come here."

Kent chuckled as he approached her. "They made it off to Sunday School then?"

"Yes they did. That is why I want to bake. Jack is no problem. He'll sleep most of the time, but when I bake, those other two marvelous children of ours can get in the way. Emmy is getting better than she was though. She's turning into quite the young lady I think." Sylvia put her arms around him, and the two embraced for a moment. "There, now I must run. Enjoy your coffee, and we'll see you two at lunch."

"Indeed you will. Again, thanks for the coffee."

Sylvia turned and nodded, "you bet."

Kent watched her as she exited the barn and then called out to Hudulak, "Hey, Alex!" he called, "Alex, there is some fresh coffee down here if you want some. Come and get it while it's hot."

"What's that, boss man?" Hudulak hollered back as he stopped scraping the stall floor with the shovel. "Boss man, did you call me?" he yelled again down the corridor.

"Yeah, Sylvia brought us some fresh coffee. Come and get a cup while it is hot."

"Coffee?" he muttered to himself. They usually didn't stop for coffee until after the first few hogs were done. "I'll be right there." It was odd, but nonetheless, he was not going to turn down a cup of hot coffee. Scooping up the last shovel load of old straw and pig scat, he tossed it into the wheelbarrow and leaned the shovel against the stall. As he made his way down the barn corridor, he could hear Kent whistling. He always did that, and he certainly knew how to carry a tune. Hudulak smiled, when Kent whistled it usually meant he was in a good mood, happy almost. Making his way over to the table, Hudulak poured himself a coffee. "Got the first stall done," he said as he put the cup to his lips.

Kent nodded and continued to whistle.

"You're a damn good whistler, boss man. Do you know that?"

Kent stopped in mid tune and smiled, "I play the harmonica too." Doing a little jig, he playfully tossed a sugar cube in the air and caught it in his mouth. "Hurry with your coffee though, there are hogs to be culled."

Hudulak, who too was in a pleasant mood, began oinking like a pig.

Kent turned and looked at him, "What was that all about?" he questioned as though Hudulak had lost his marbles.

"I'm calling the pigs. You said there was hogs that needing calling," Hudulak chuckled as he finished his coffee.

Even Kent saw the humor, and he smiled as he went back to check the temperature of the water in the tank. "Another half hour or so and the water will be hot enough to start," he said as he looked over to Hudulak.

"All right, I'll get that last stall cleaned. By then I guess it'll be time to get messy." He said with enthusiasm as he rubbed his hands together in excitement, he could hardly wait to get his hands bloodied. Gleefully he made his way to the last stall and began cleaning it. His heart raced with excitement at the thought of the impending hog slaughter. He could hardly contain the smile on his face. The thought of sticking the hogs with his knife and the emitted smell and warmth of the blood as it spewed over his hand aroused him.

For one reason or another, his mind drifted to his younger days, when he once changed his sister's diaper, and for reason only known to him spread her legs to far apart, making her cry. He remembered how brutally his mother beat him after that with a broom handle until his back bore welts and bruises. He had hated authoritative women ever since. He thought of them when he thought about the hogs he was about to kill. Scraping up the last straw and manure, he tossed it into the wheelbarrow, and dumped it on the pile outside. Rubbing his hands together to warm them up as the cold nipped at them, he smiled. *There, now for the real fun,* he thought.

Chapter 7

Kent and Hudulak were relieved when the last hog was hanging with the others. "Whew. That was a good day," Kent said as he wiped his brow, and looked at Hudulak. "It sure was. We still have a heck of a lot of clean up. Plus, I imagine you want the hogs loaded up in the truck." "Well, the worst part is over," Kent inhaled, tiredly. "We can slow the pace down when we clean. Maybe we should have a short rest for now." Reaching into his pocket, he pulled out his pipe and tobacco.

"I suppose that is a good idea, I'm a bit beat too, a short rest sounds good to me." Hudulak moved closer to Kent who was standing near the boiler absorbing the heat. "Thirty hogs in two days. Not bad, I'd say. They look better hanging than when they're alive. Don't stink as bad either," Hudulak half smiled.

Kent took a long draw from his pipe and exhaled. "The stink is going to be tenfold come next year when we have more hogs. It is all part of the job. I have been thinking, you know, that maybe we should build a bigger corral than the one that we have now. It would have to be high enough to keep out the dogs and coyotes. We could put the hogs out in herds of twenty on a daily basis throughout the spring and summer." Kent smiled, "See, I told you that you would be busy."

"I'd rather be busy than not. I can't earn a wage if I don't work. To keep the hounds and coyotes out, a ten-foot-high corral would probably be best, I think. We could put in eight by eight by twelve foot timbers in the corners. When those suckers are in two feet deep, they'll never move. Heck, you'd be able to build a damn good corral. It would be good for horses and such too."

"That is a good idea, Alex, rather than looking at that later, and wishing we had done it right in the first place. I was thinking only of the hogs, but, its better being prepared

for the day I get a few horses or a couple of milk cows."
Kent was nodding his head in deep thought. "I'll call around
over the next week to see about getting timbers from one of
the local sawmills. They always give you a better price than
Harper's Lumber."

"Is Harper's Lumber the only lumber yard around?"
Hudulak asked, with curiosity.

"They are yep, but they have to order the timbers and
planks that we want, they don't carry much of it. It would be
as quick, if not quicker, if I order from one of the mills."

Just then, the 2x4-door latch slid off its saddle, and the
barn door creaked open. It was Sylvia with the kids in tow.

"Wow! Look who the barn cat let in," Kent said as he
smiled at them. Jack was snuggled in Sylvia's arms. The first
thing he did was wrinkle up his nose at the smell from the
barn.

"What is a matter Jack?" Kent asked as he tickled his son
under the chin.

"Eeeww Daddy, you haven't even washed your hands,"
Emily said as she moved out of his way to avoid the same.

Richard laughed. "You are such a sissy Emmy. Tickle my
chin Dad," he said as he stuck out his chin. Of course, Kent
could not resist. Richard laughed even louder as Kent
pretended to chase Emily.

"Stop it Daddy, or I won't let you have any of the cookies
Mommy helped me bake for you."

"What? You baked cookies for us. Well then, I guess I
better stop."

"Yes, you'd better because they are very good cookies,"
Emily stated, with her hands on her hips.

"All right, you win," Kent, responded.

"Thank you Daddy. When will you smelly men come to
the house?" she asked. "I want you to have some of those
cookies while they are still fresh."

"An hour or so, I imagine. Unless, you all want to chip in
and help us clean," her father teased.

"No way, Daddy, I don't want to help. I don't like the look of the guts."

"Don't look at me, Kent. Jack and I can't help. I have dinner cooking," Sylvia added.

"Then that leaves only you, Richard. Do you want to help us clean up?"

"Um, I dunno. What can I do?" Richard shrugged his shoulders.

"Well, Alex and you could clean the stalls where the hogs were."

"Sure, I'd like to have a hand doing that, and I think Richard is the right fellow to help," Hudulak said, with a smile.

"Okay. Is that okay, Mom?" he asked.

"I don't see why not. Make sure you wear a pair of your father's gloves. And don't forget to wash up afterward."

"I won't. What do you want me to do Alex?"

"We'll need the water hose and a couple of shovels. You can get those. I'll meet you down at the last stall."

"Okay. Cool! I get to help dad and Alex," Richard said as he stuck his tongue out at Emily. He went to the water hose, and began unrolling it and stretching it out.

"Dad, where are your gloves?"

Kent reached into his back pocket and handed Richard a pair.

"These will do."

"Thanks Dad," Taking the gloves he slipped them on, "They sure are big," he said.

"You have to have some kind of movement in them to keep the fingers warm."

A glow of pride lit up Kent's face, and he smiled.

"If you work hard, I'll pay you a quarter."

"A whole quarter?" Richard asked, excitedly.

"Yep, but you have to listen to Alex."

"I will." With that, Richard darted down the corridor to the last set of stalls. "Hey, Alex, dad is going to pay me a quarter for helping you!"

"A whole quarter?" Hudulak asked.

"Yeah, I asked him that too, and he said 'yep'."

Hudulak chuckled. "That is pretty good pay for a young whippersnapper like you."

"I'll be able to buy a squirt gun and maybe some candy too."

"You don't need any candy do you?" Hudulak asked as the two of them started cleaning.

"I like candy, but I probably don't need any, and mom might not allow me to have any."

Hudulak wanted to tell him that if he earned the money, then *no woman* should tell him how he could or could not spend it. It made Hudulak angry as he thought back to his own controlling mother. Instead, he held his tongue.

"Maybe stick with the squirt gun," he responded.

"I'll buy Jack and Emily one too. That would make them happy."

"Jack, maybe, Emily not so much," Hudulak responded.

"You are probably right. She likes coloring and dolls. I could buy her some coloring pencils," Richard said as he stopped for a moment and thought. "Yeah, I think that is what I will do."

"I'll tell you what Richard. I'll pay you a quarter too for helping me. That should be enough money to buy those things."

"Wowee! Will you truly?"

"I sure will. I'll pay you tonight when we get back to the house."

"I'll have two quarters. That would buy a lot of candy. How many monies is that Alex?"

"Monies? It is not monies, Richard. It is money. It would be fifty cents. That is a pretty good wage for helping us out," Hudulak was smiling. He liked Richard, not because they shared a name but because Richard was a bright little fellow. He was always willing to help, and although he wasn't always allowed to do so, the desire was there.

"I only get one of those monies a week. That's what dad pays us for an allowance."

Hudulak stopped working and leaned on his shovel, "One of those 'what'?" he questioned with a smile.

"Money, I only get that much money a week," Richard corrected.

Hudulak smiled and nodded. "That's better. Look at that, Richard. We are almost done. A couple shovel loads and that will be it. Then, you can turn the hose on and spray out this stall and that one," he pointed to the stall he had cleaned earlier.

"Okay Alex." Richard heaved a shovel full of manure into the wheelbarrow. "Whew, that one was heavy. I think it is full now."

"One or two more and I'll dump it. You get the hose now," Hudulak said as he carried on cleaning the stall.

Richard leaned his shovel against the stall wall.

"Nope, don't put that there," Hudulak, ordered. "Put it back where you got it. That way, we'll always know where it is. Everything has its place, and every place has its thing. That's how I remember to put things back."

"My dad would tell me the same thing, probably," Richard smiled, as he grabbed the shovel. "He doesn't even like it when we leave our toys out."

Hudulak once more stopped and leaned on his shovel. "Well, you wouldn't want to lose any of the toys would you?"

"No sir. I wouldn't want that."

"That's right, and that's the way you want to keep tools too. If you put them back and tidy up, you'll never lose a one."

Richard nodded as he contemplated the lesson. "Yeah that makes sense. Tools probably cost more than toys," he said as he walked away to get the hose and to put the shovel back.

By 6:00 o'clock that evening, they were finally finished with the cleaning. Sylvia, Emily, and Jack had long been gone back to the house. Tossing a few pieces of scrap to the family dog, Kent smiled at Richard. Digging into his pocket, he pulled out a couple of dimes and a nickel. "Here is the wage I promised. That was a job well done Richard."

"Thanks Dad. Alex is going to pay me too, so I'll have fifty cents," Richard was gloating with pride, and he smiled as he ran ahead.

"Save it up, and in a while you might have enough to buy a piglet yourself. You'd double your money and then some."

"How much would I make Dad?" he was curious now as he slowed down and turned back.

"Well, let's see," Kent, thought for a moment. "One piglet might cost you ten dollars. Then you would have to pay for its keep."

"You mean like for feed and stuff?"

"That's right. So, when it is all said and done, you might walk away with a twenty dollar profit, maybe a wee bit more."

Richard was ecstatic at hearing this and his interest grew even deeper. "Wow! I could buy a lot of stuff with twenty dollars."

"You could, or you could buy another piglet or two."

"Yeah, then I would keep making money. I have a lot to think about."

"Yep," Kent replied as he opened the barn door and the three of them exited.

"I might buy a couple too," Hudulak stated. "I guess you and I both have some thinking to do, eh?"

"Uhuh, I like farming," Richard said with enthusiasm as he skipped ahead once more.

"I think the little fellow is going to buy a hog, boss man."

The two of them watched Richard speed ahead and reach up to unlock the barnyard gate. "Hurry up you guys. I have to tell mom that I'm going to buy a piggy," Richard called out as he opened the gate.

"We're right behind you Richard," Kent replied. "About the buying of a hog, you haven't even thought about it for more than five minutes. It isn't a decision you should make so quick. Think about it for a day or two."

"Yeah, your dad is right Ricky. I haven't made my decision yet either."

Richard hung his head knowing that his dad and Alex were right. It was a decision he should not make so quickly. "All right, I guess I'll think on it, but I'm pretty sure."

"Sometimes, when we make a decision in haste we forget the reality of it. If you buy a pig, it will be your responsibility to keep it fed, just as you do with the rabbits. It isn't easy, son."

"Could my pig have his own pen? I am pretty sure I could keep one clean," Richard was sincere as he said that.

Kent chuckled, "I don't doubt that you could. Still, it is hard work. I'll tell you what," he began as he closed and locked the gate. "I'll ask you again on Friday. That is almost a week away. If you still want a pig then you can have one. If you decide not to get one, we'll go into town that Saturday, and you can buy whatever you want."

"Whatever I want?" Richard looked up to his father for reassurance that indeed he could buy whatever he wanted.

"Yep, whatever you want and can afford." There was a reason Kent made the offer. With whatever decision Richard made, he would learn a valuable financial lesson. If he decided to buy a pig, he would get a return of some kind. If he decided to spend his money, there would be no return whatsoever. In his opinion, it was a good lesson either way. Deep down he did want Richard to raise a hog. The boy was young but not young enough to be useless. Perhaps encouraging him to make decisions at such a young age, whether right or wrong, was a good idea.

"Wow. I can't wait until Friday."

"Well then, you better keep them shiny coins in your piggy bank. You wouldn't want to lose them."

"No, I wouldn't. It is like putting the tools away, right Alex?" Richard looked up to Hudulak who was smiling.

"That is for sure."

By now, they reached the house. Richard was first with his boots off. Kent and Hudulak sat on the porch bench slowly removing theirs. Their backs ached and their feet hurt.

"I'm sure glad that is finally done, boss man. It was harder than I thought it would be."

"What's that, taking off your boots or slaughtering the hogs?" Kent joked.

Hudulak laughed, "Well, put that way, both were tough. Feels like my feet have swollen to twice their size."

"Mine too, that's what happens when you stand all day. I can't wait to clean up, have dinner, and sit in my chair. Maybe listen to the late news on CBC."

"What about the hogs hanging in the barn? Are we going to load them into the truck tonight or tomorrow?"

"I'll make arrangements with Dackers to have them dropped off tomorrow. You and Sylvia can deliver a load in the morning. It's better to hang them over night than to load them in the truck." With that, Kent stretched, and made his way up the two stairs of the porch to the kitchen foyer. "Hey hon, we're finished for the year! It sure brings a smile to my face." He went to Sylvia and planted a kiss on her cheek. Hudulak catching this from the corner of his eye felt a surge of jealousy. He wanted nothing more than to be the one kissing her. Lowering his head, he made his way past the two entwined lovers to the room he shared with the boys. He removed his butchering clothes and wrapped a towel around his waist, picked out a clean set of clothes and headed for the shower.

The hot water felt good on his sweaty skin as he scrubbed. The taste of salt in his mouth told him that he had once again bit a hole in his cheek. That often happened when he thought of women. He hated them and desired them at the same time. He could never understand that about himself. He had very few relationships that were a success. Actually, the only way he could relate to women was to get them drunk. Then, meaningless sex transpired.

Long-term relationships were unattainable for Hudulak. The reasons for that related to his looks, his mannerisms, and his false state of mind. He practiced for years on fooling people in different ways for different things. It was one skill, he had. More often than not, he blamed some of his past problems on alcohol. He blamed other problems on his epilepsy. He was remarkably adept when it came to fooling people. Refreshed, he stepped out of the shower.

He wiped the steamed-up mirror and looked deep into his own eyes. Seeing Kent and Sylvia embraced as they were, reminded him that it was three months since he last slept with a woman. He needed a weekend off in one of the nearby cities. He knew the type of town that Trail was. There were women on the prowl who would sleep with him for a couple of dollars or a few drinks. That was always the best way. Hudulak smiled to himself. *If only I could have my way with Sylvia,* he thought.

There was a knock on the door.

"Are you going to be much longer, Alex?" Kent asked. "I need to clean up myself."

"Nope, I'm all done now, boss man. I'll be out in a minute." He was a little embarrassed at where his hand was, and was grateful Kent had not opened the door. *Damn, I'll have to finish later.* Dressing into his clean clothes, he looked down at his crotch to make sure there was no visible bulge between his legs. Satisfied, he opened the door and headed to the kitchen, "All yours boss man," he said as he as he headed to the kitchen and poured himself a coffee. Sylvia sat alone at the table in the dining room and so he made his way there.

"Sure feels good to be clean again," Hudulak said as he sat down at his usual spot at the table.

"I bet it does. Both of you were pretty messy," Sylvia replied.

"Well, in my defense, I'm still learning the ins and outs of hog harvesting. It'll be a lot cleaner next year." He took a sip from his coffee. God, Sylvia looked good to him, the way she sat there. Although she was an authoritative woman, and usually he hated that in women, she had a way of making authority look sexy.

"Kent has been doing it for a few years already, and I can tell you that it doesn't get any cleaner."

"Probably not, especially if next season there are a hundred or more that need butchering."

"That's the goal. I hope we can afford it."

"Ah, don't worry about that, boss lady. You folks will do all right. Pork prices are up a bit, and I bet a lot of them will weigh out nice and plump. Kent is hoping for six thousand pounds of swinging pork, but I think he is going to get a surprise, I say he'll have that, plus some. It will be a good payout for you folks." Hudulak brought his cup to his lips and took a swallow.

"I suppose," Sylvia started, "Still, there are our feed costs, maintenance cost and your wage. It all adds up, but I think you are right Alex. We will do well this year."

"I bet so, yep, I'm glad I was able to put you at ease a bit," he smiled at her. "Where did Emily and the boys get to? I haven't seen them since getting out of the shower," he asked.

"Jack is asleep. Emily and Richard are playing quietly in our bedroom."

"Oh," Hudulak rose from the table to pour himself another coffee. "Can I get you another coffee too, boss lady?"

"No thanks Alex, but, thank you for asking," Sylvia looked out the big picture window, although it was early evening, the darkening sky was a sure sign that the days were getting shorter.

Making his way back to the table with coffee in hand, Hudulak too looked out the window and shivered as a chill ran up his spine. He thought about the upcoming winter and how much he loathed it. The snow and Christmas were the two things he hated most of all. The cold didn't bother him much, but the snow was a different story. He had no fond memories of winters past. In his youth, Christmas was rarely celebrated his family was poor, and there was no reason to be joyful.

As an adult, he would spend Christmas with his hand wrapped around a bottle, and drink until he could drink no more. When he finally sobered up, the holiday season would be over. He would have to fake it this year. Kent seemed to be a bit of a stickler when it came to drinking. The last thing he wanted was to get on his bad side.

He liked Kent; he was straightforward and hard working. In Hudulak's opinion, Kent was a wee-bit religious. That was probably the only thing he did not like about him. He liked everything about Sylvia. "It seems darker tonight than it did last night at the same time, doesn't it?" he asked as he turned his head to look at her.

"Yes it does, it is getting to be that time of the year, mind you. Have you ever been on a horse-drawn sled?" she asked out of blue, as she remembered her own youth.

"Nope, I don't like horses much boss lady and they don't like me."

"You have worked on ranches and mixed farms before. How could you not like horses," she responded.

"Yeah, I've worked with horses and such, but that doesn't mean I like them. I'm not sure why I don't like them, but for one reason or another I don't," Hudulak took a sip from his coffee.

"When I grew up as a kid on the prairie, we used to have a sled that we hooked up to the horses. My father would collect all the neighbor kids, and off we would go. It is a part of my childhood that, I remember well, boy, it was fun. I tried to convince Kent to buy a horse or two and sled, but he is not interested in that yet. He said, 'maybe in a few years.' I would like to keep up the tradition and pass it onto our kids, but it is up to Kent. He is too busy with hogs right now."

"I guess it could've been fun. Doesn't sound like much fun to me, though."

"Don't be like that," Sylvia said with a smile. "Tell me something about your childhood."

"Like what?"

"I don't know. You must remember something good, fun, or special. Everyone does."

The more he listened to her talk the more he wished he did have something to say; but he actually didn't. There was nothing to tell. In fact, his childhood had been a total disaster. He tried to think of something to say, but there was nothing there.

"Not me. My childhood was ordinary. The only good memory I have is when I finally left home in my teens. My mother was a bit of a tyrant if you know what I mean. As for my dad, I never knew him, and my mother never spoke of him."

"That is terrible."

Hudulak waved his hand through the air, "Ah, you learn to live with it."

Just then, Kent walked in all freshened up and shaved. "Learn to live with what?" he asked, wanting to join in on the conversation.

64

"We were talking about our childhood. I was telling Alex about the sled we had when I grew up, and how I want us to have one eventually. You know, to keep the tradition going."

"Yeah, we will work on that sooner or later," he liked the idea. It always sounded like fun whenever Sylvia described it, but he knew the cost it could entail, and he was not prepared to handle it yet. In time, Sylvia would have her sled.

"Now that I'm all washed up, where are these cookies Emmy made?" he asked as he made his way into the kitchen.

"The fresh batch is in last year's Christmas cookie tin. Bring in a plate of them Kent. I'm sure Emmy would want Alex to try some."

"Yes, I would like to try some of Emmy's cookies. I bet she did a real good job on them."

There was a bit of rattling going on in the kitchen. Finally, Kent returned, a plate of cookies in one hand and a coffee in the other. "They sure look good, don't they," he said as he set the plate down. "The coffee is a bit old, but it'll do. Help yourself to the cookies, Alex." Kent sat next to Sylvia at the table, and the three of them chatted about their work and Kent's plans. An hour later, they made their way into the living room, and Kent took his harmonica off the shelf. Calling for Richard and Emily, he sat down in his chair. Within minutes, the sweet sound of his harmonica echoed through the Townsend home.

Sylvia and the children clapped to the beat while Hudulak sat quietly. His depression was due to being in the presence of a happy family, something had never experienced. He felt deprived, saddened, and jealous. Excusing himself, he bid them all good night, and retreated to the solitude of his room. He felt better being away from them. *Let them enjoy their happiness,* he thought as he closed his eyes.

Chapter 8

He was up at the same time as Kent the following morning. It was the beginning of a new week. They met in the dining room and discussed what Kent wanted him to do that day. There was a bit of cleanup to be done and he wanted him to load the truck with some of the pigs they butchered. Kent was going to take the car to work. He wanted the first load taken that morning. Sylvia would drive the truck once Emily was off to school, and Richard and Jack were, dropped off at the neighbors. The second load could wait until he got home from work that evening.

"That's easy enough, boss man." Hudulak chewed a mouthful of eggs and toast. He felt a little rush knowing that the two boys were going to be away all day. He would be alone with Sylvia and might have a chance to spy on her. That thought alone aroused him.

"Not sure it'll be that easy, but I know you can handle it. Pace yourself though, work smart. Loading sixty half-sides of pork can get tiring. You can have a short rest while Sylvia drives into town, unless you tag along. It doesn't matter to me, as long as the work is done. Anyway," Kent finished as he looked at his watch, "I've got to hit the road. I'll see you later." He rose from the table and set his breakfast dishes in the sink.

Hudulak watched as he pulled out onto the dirt road and the taillights disappeared. The house was silent, and for a moment, he stood at the kitchen window looking out. The sun was barely making an appearance yet, but there was work to do. He put the dishes in the sink, slipped on his boots, and headed outside. He thought about parking the truck down by the barn until he remembered that Sylvia would need it to drop off the kids. "I'll get it later, I guess," he said to himself as he made his way to the barnyard gate. The dog ran in front of him, and he playfully kicked a rock at it. "How is it going today, you old hound?" he asked as the dog ran further ahead.

He opened the gate and made his way to the barn. It was surprisingly warm inside as compared to the chill outside. The silence struck him as odd. Usually thirty hogs were squealing whenever he stepped inside. Today though, their bodies hung from barn rafters in silence. He looked them over making sure nothing had gone awry. A quirky smile crossed his face as he relived their slaughter. It was as though he knew each one personally. Each of their deaths documented in recesses of his mind. He remembered how that one squealed, or how that one bled, and how another one continued to squeal and run after he had put a bullet in its head. They were trophies in his mind.

"I bet a woman would squeal and bleed like you stinky suckers too," he said to himself as he stepped back to look at them again.

"You stinking swine look like women that have been drawn and quartered, I'm guessing," he observed.

It was a time when he could be himself. When he was with the family, he was smart enough to keep his thoughts to himself. Alone he could say and do anything. Some things would have been disturbing to Kent or Sylvia. Feeling the urge, he made his way to the first stall in the long corridor of the barn. A few weeks earlier, he had found a bunch of old Eaton's catalogues that Kent had used to start the boiler. He sat on a straw bale, unzipped his fly, and looked through the catalogue. After a few minutes, he was relieved of his sexual stress, and he put the catalogue away.

Two hours later, while Sylvia stood by, he began to load the truck with the first of the swinging pork. He rested every now and again to converse with her.

"Sure is a nice day out," Hudulak said as he wiped his brow, "compared to the early morning chill, that is."

"Yes. The sun is sure bright and hot today. I love the early fall. Spring, too, is one of my favorite times."

"I'm a spring and fall man myself. I find the summers too hot, and well, winter is a different story. I don't like the snow, to say the least. I can live with the cold, but can do without the snow."

"That seems strange for someone who lived up North."

"That's probably why I don't like it," he smiled. "Now, winters in Alberta, that's a different story too. I lived there a couple of times. It could get brutally cold one minute and the next a warm southwest wind could pick up. That is what they call a Chinook down that way isn't it?"

"It sure is. I liked that about Alberta too."

"I kind of miss the place," Hudulak said as he reminisced. "Anyway, I guess I should get back at it. I've rested enough for now. Talk to you later, boss lady," he said with a smile as he turned, and headed back to the barn.

Sylvia waited as he entered; then she slipped into the hay barn, and checked on the rabbits.

"Hello there, you fuzzy creatures, how are you doing today?" she asked as she checked their food and water. "I guess you could use fresh water and more feed. I'll bring you down some greens from last night later on, or Emily and Richard will."

She opened the cage door and retrieved the rabbits feed and water dishes. She neglected to close the cage door all the way, when she left. When she returned with fresh water and feed, the furry critters darted this way and that as she entered that part of the hay barn.

"Oh my God!" she yelled, in surprise. "Alex! Help!" she screamed as she tried to round up the felons.

With a half side of pork draped across his shoulder, Hudulak quickened his pace and tossed it into the truck. "What's the matter?" he called as he ran across the barnyard and opened the door.

"The rabbits have gotten out," Sylvia said in exasperation as she knelt on the floor trying to catch them.

"How in the world did that happen?"

"I guess I didn't close the cage properly."

"We're not going to catch them by scaring them. The barn door is closed, so they aren't getting outside. Calm down for a minute and let them settle," Hudulak said as he politely and *seemingly inadvertently* touched her breast as he helped her up. "Sorry about that, boss lady."

"No worries Alex, it was an accident. So, how long will it take these rabbits to calm down?" she asked as she dusted off her knees.

"A few minutes, I'm glad this happened to you and not me. Boss man would be real upset if it was me or the boy," Alex said, referring to Richard.

"They're only rabbits. How upset would he actually get?"

Hudulak shrugged. "I don't know. Might not say a thing, or he might."

"We'll have them back where they belong before he comes home. Don't worry so much Alex. Besides it is my fault and if he wants to have hot dinners for the rest of the week, he'll know better than to give me a hard time," Sylvia smiled.

Hudulak chuckled. "Since you put it that way, this is pretty funny." There was a short pause, "I think what we should do is slip out and close the door. They aren't going to settle much with us looming over them. By the time I finish loading the pork, they'll have calmed enough. It will give me something to do while you are in town. The pork is the priority at this time."

"Okay. I want you to know I am sorry this happened though."

"Think nothing of it, boss lady." Hudulak opened the door and gestured for her to step out. As she passed by him, he watched her closely. She looked so good; he wanted to gobble her up. Stepping out he gently closed the door. "Do you know what time it is getting to be?" he asked.

Sylvia pulled her shirtsleeve to reveal her dainty wrist, and cream-colored rose petal scented skin.

"It is almost 11:30. That reminds me. I made some sandwiches for you. I hope you aren't sick of chicken salad. You can help yourself to some of Emmy's cookies. There is iced tea in the refrigerator."

"Chicken salad sounds good to me and iced tea too. I need to finish loading up these hog carcasses first, only got a couple more to go."

A few minutes later Sylvia was on her way to town, and Hudulak was on his way to the house for lunch. The rabbits could wait. He removed his boots and washed his hands at the kitchen sink. He looked around the empty house. It was silent except for the sound of his breathing. It was the first time since working for the Townsends that he was alone in their house.

His heart raced as he ate lunch. It seemed odd and unfamiliar. Usually Jack sat across from him. Most of the time, he would pick up his lunch and sit at the table outside before heading back to the barn. Usually he ate his lunch in a rush. Today was different and he took his time, savoring every mouthful of his chicken salad sandwich.

His mind drifted from reality to fantasy as he began to think of Sylvia. He felt anger towards Kent for being married to her, and rage against himself for the lack of the looks or demeanor to attract such a woman. He slammed his fist into the table in a brief show of anger. As with all his tantrums, his anger eased away, and the rage subsided.

I could have my way with her if I really wanted... I know I could, he thought as he took a sip of his iced tea. *Someday, when Kent is on the late shift, I'll get her drunk. Then we'll see how far I can get.*

A smile crossed his face as he stood from the table and made his way into their bedroom where he rummaged through Sylvia's underwear. He became aroused as he looked at her frilly clothing. He spent some time satisfying his arousal, and then put the undergarments back in the drawer arranged as he had found them. With his heart beating fast from the sexual release, he made his way to his boots and headed back to the barn.

By the time Sylvia returned from town that day, he had rounded up all the wily rabbits and put them back in their cage. He was sitting in the shade on a straw bale when she pulled up. He rose and opened the gate for her.

"How did it go?" he asked as he waved her in.

Sylvia rolled down her window to reply.

"Those thirty half-sides weighed out close to three thousand pounds. The butcher is going to pay us forty-two cents a pound. The average hog weighed near two-hundred pounds," she said with glee as she moved the truck ahead.

Stepping out she smiled.

"They weighed out nicely, Alex, as you predicted!"

"Boss man is going to be happy about that. His three-hundred dollar investment is going to give him about twenty-five hundred. That is pretty good I'd say."

"Close, yes. Do you have time to have a short break?"

"In case you didn't notice, I was sitting down over there when you pulled up," he pointed toward the straw bale. "I ran out of work a while ago. Got the rabbits back in their cage, and the stalls in the barn are clean as whistles. I'd say I have time for a short break."

"That straw bale looks like as good a place as any, to sit down for a bit," Sylvia replied, as the two of them walked over to it.

"I never really took notice how nice this place is." Hudulak began as they sat down. He wanted to make conversation.

"It is exceptionally beautiful. We did well buying here."

"I wouldn't argue that. Someday I hope to have a place like this of my own." He paused for a moment as he daydreamed. "Except, I'm not sure where that might be." It was a pipe dream, and he knew it.

"There are all kinds of beautiful places I could live, if not here." Sylvia began, "there are parts of Alberta and

Saskatchewan that are lovely. I have even seen pictures of the North. It too, is extremely pretty."

"I haven't seen much of Saskatchewan, but I do like Alberta. As a kid before we moved north, we lived in Faust, a farming community. Maybe I'll return there when the time comes."

"How long did you live there, Alex?"

"I don't think I was older than ten when we moved. It seems so long ago."

"Does some of your family live there?"

"Not as far as I know. I have a younger sister, but we don't speak. I haven't heard from anyone in my family in years. I like it that way. They stay out of my business, and I stay out of theirs."

Sylvia was beginning to believe his imaginative stories, and, in a way, she felt sad for him. "That sounds terrible Alex."

"Not really, when you know how much we hate each other," he smiled and rose. "I guess I better get started in loading up the rest of the butchering. It was nice having a chat with you, boss lady."

"It was enjoyable talking to you too. Thanks for rounding up the rabbits." Sylvia went towards the house, and Hudulak watched from the screen-covered barn window. *One day I will see more of you than I do now,* he thought.

He loaded the last of the hog carcasses. It took the better part of an hour to finish. While leaning against the truck tailgate, he looked towards Hudu Creek. He smiled when he spotted a White Tail buck jump the fence and cross the field followed by three does. *There is a lucky bastard,* he thought. He watched until they vanished into the darkening wood.

Covering the hogs with a tarp to keep the flies off he went to the barn. A few stalls could use some minor repairs. There were loose hinges and broken boards to keep him busy until Kent arrived home in an hour or so.

Armed with a hammer, a handsaw, and a tin full of nails, he began making the repairs using old boards stacked alongside the barn. The hour dragged on as he worked. He felt that he had been at it forever. It didn't help when it began to get bitterly cold. Even inside the barn, he could feel the chill in the air. The wind picked up from the North, bringing with it dark ominous clouds. The sun now shrouded by the dark grey clouds, he stepped outside and looked up to the sky.

It is going to rain or snow, he thought as he shivered. *That sure moved in fast.* Shrugging his shoulders, he gathered up his tools, and made a final check to be sure that he didn't forget anything. The few stalls that he repaired looked good and he was satisfied. He, nodded to himself, y*ep I earned my wage today, too.*

By the time he put the tools away, he could hear Kent's car coming down the road. He stepped out of the barn as it was pulling into the driveway. "There he is," he muttered as he closed the barn door and headed to the house. He came up as Kent was pulling off his boots.

"Good afternoon, boss man."

"Hello, Alex. Did you manage to keep busy today?"

"Sure did. The last of the hogs are loaded and ready for the butcher."

"Good, we will get to it in a bit. Right now I want a coffee and a sit down."

"I'll join you."

"By all means."

"It was a good day, boss man. That is, of course until the clouds moved in. It was sunny most of the day."

"When I left work, the sun was still shining in Trail. In fact, it was sunny right until I got to this side of Fruitvale. I think the storm will pass. We might get a few drops of rain or maybe some hail," he replied as he waited for Hudulak to remove his boots.

The two made their way to the kitchen and a fresh cup of coffee.

Sylvia was sitting at the dining room table.

"Hello, hon. How was your day?" she asked.

"Same old, same old, let's say that I'm glad to be home." Kent bent down and kissed her cheek. "How was yours?"

"Interesting, to say the least, did Alex mention what the first load of hogs weighed?"

"Nope, I didn't. I figured it was your place to say. Not mine."

"So, what did they weigh?" Kent asked.

"The first load was a little bit less than three thousand pounds, and Dackers is going to pay us forty-two cents a pound. I bet that makes your day, doesn't it?"

"That is good. Wow! Yes, that does make my day," he smiled as he sat down. "No point in figuring out our return yet. It would only be speculation." He took a sip of his coffee. "We'll get to that later. Where are the kids? Are they still at the neighbors?"

"Yes. Emily came home and got out of her school clothes before she went there. I told her that we would pick them up before dinner."

"It is almost 4:00 o'clock now, Alex and I will finish our coffee then head into town with the last load. You could take the car, and get the kids if we aren't back in time. You know how Dackers is. He will want to talk, that man could wear out one's ears." There was a short pause as Kent inhaled deeply. "Anyway, he expects us around 4:30. He warned me that there might be a few others ahead of us. I hope that is not the case, but it could be. If we are not back by 5:30, you and the kids might as well go ahead and eat. Alex and I can pick something up in town."

"Good thing I'm only heating up the leftover chicken and some vegetables. Maybe I'll make chicken sandwiches instead if you guys aren't back by then."

"Could you save me enough for lunch tomorrow, boss lady? I'd appreciate that."

"Of course I will Alex. No worries."

"Thanks," Hudulak said as he finished the last of his coffee. "I'm all done. I'll meet you down at the barn boss man." He rose from the table and set his empty cup in the sink.

"Hey, Alex," Kent called after him. "Go ahead and bring the truck to the house. I'll meet you outside. The keys are in the truck." He paused for a second and looked at Sylvia. "They are, aren't they?"

Sylvia nodded, 'yes' that they were.

"No problem." Hudulak slipped back into the porch and pulled his boots on. The sun still had not broken through the clouds. In the distance, the dark clouds seemed even darker than earlier. *Shit, looks like we're going to get a rainstorm for sure,* he thought as he walked to the barn. He was annoyed when he discovered that the keys were not in the ignition. "Damn it."

He felt flustered. It had already been a long day, and while he was making his way back to the house, the rain started. It came down in torrents. He ran the last few yards, and when he poked his head into the kitchen foyer, he saw that Sylvia was sitting on Kent's lap, and they were laughing and kissing. Embarrassed, he slipped back into the porch and waited a few minutes. Then, he opened the porch door and closed it a bit louder so that they could hear him.

"Hey, boss man," he called out as he peeked through the kitchen doorway. "The keys aren't in the truck."

Sylvia slipped off Kent's lap and reached into her jacket pocket. "I'm so sorry, Alex. I thought I left them in the truck. Here they are," she said as she handed them to him.

"That's okay. We should have brought the truck to the house earlier. Thanks." Taking the keys from her, he headed back out the door. "Stupid," he muttered as he walked towards the barn.

75

Already soaked to the core it did not matter if he ran or walked. Either way he would need dry clothes before they headed into town. He opened the driver side door, slid in, slammed the key into the ignition, started the motor, and headed towards the house, just stopping to close the gate behind him. He was grateful the old truck was an automatic. He was not any good at shifting gears with a three on the tree transmission. In fact, he had driven a standard only once or twice and hated it every time. He parked and went into the house. Kent was sitting on the porch bench putting on his boots.

"Have to change my clothes; it's raining cats and dogs. I'm soaked to the bone. I'll only be a minute, boss man."

"Go ahead. We have a few minutes before we have to leave," Kent replied as he tied his boots up. "I'll meet you in the truck."

"Okay, boss man." A few minutes later, after slipping into some dry clothes, he ran to the truck and the two of them headed into town. The road was muddy and they fish tailed a few times. That perked up Hudulak's spirit, and he hollered, "Yee Haw!"

"You seem chipper today," Kent was smiling himself as he looked over to him.

"It was a good day, boss man. That is until this damn rain came." There was a pause as they concentrated on the road, trying to avoid the bigger ruts in it that were now filling with rain. "Gee, the old road sure sops up the water, good thing it isn't all up hill. We'd be slipping and sliding the whole way."

"Whether it is up hill or not, we have to keep our wits about us. The road to Fruitvale has washed out a time or two when it has rained this hard. The wipers are barely keeping the rain off now."

"It is quite the storm that's for sure." The two fell silent as they watched and listened to the sounds of rain and the thunder in the distance. "I'm glad that you are driving, boss man. I never cared about driving in stuff like this. I mean, I would drive if I had too."

"I've driven the road so often I know where all the bad parts are." Kent slowed down and put the truck in second gear. "You only have to be careful and pay attention. Sometimes a prayer isn't such a terrible idea," Kent said.

"Ah, I don't turn to prayer much. I'm not sure I believe all that mumble jumble."

"You must believe in something?"

"Yeah I do, hard work. If a man wants something, he can get it. He doesn't have to pray for it. Just work hard." Hudulak looked out the window as he tried to make himself believe that is how it was.

"To each his own I suppose. That is a good point though. Hard work is what makes the world go around." Kent felt the need to have a smoke. He was driving slowly enough, and they hadn't made the main road yet. Reaching into his shirt pocket, he pulled out his pipe and filled it with tobacco. Putting it to his lips, he lit a match and inhaled the pungent smoke. "Ahh, that's better," he said as he exhaled, and puffed some more as he rolled down the window to let the smoke out. "Have you ever smoked Alex?"

"Once in a while I do, especially when I'm having a beer. I haven't had a pouch of cigarette tobacco for a long time. Maybe I'll pick up a pouch."

"I prefer a pipe, but, I think both habits are filthy. Sometimes I wish I never started. I tried quitting a couple of times, but, here I am smoking," Kent said as they continued.

"That is tough to do. I guess I'm lucky because I can go without if I want to and it doesn't bother me."

A bolt of lightning that lit up the sky was immediately, followed by a loud crack of thunder. It startled the two.

"Man that was close, eh?"

"I almost dumped my pipe all over myself. It certainly was loud." Kent looked up to the sky. "It isn't going to let up either, not until these clouds blow further to the East.

They're headed that way now. Maybe it will stop before we get back to the farm. Sure, hope it does, the barn yard turns into a mess when it rains like this."

Chapter 9

The main road to town was slick and slippery most of the way. They arrived in time to meet with Dackers at 4:30.

"That is a nice load of hogs you have, Kent. I can tell by how low your truck is riding. Your wife brought a nice load too. You did well this year, I think."

"I hope so, by the way, I don't think you have met Alex. He's the fellow that I hired to help around the farm," Kent said as he introduced the two.

"Nice to meet you, Alex," Dackers smiled.

"Right back at you," Hudulak, replied as the two of them shook hands.

"Let's get these hogs unloaded, I'm sure you want to get home," Dackers said as he helped remove the tarp. "Indeed, those are nice looking," he said as he lifted one. "We'll get them inside and weigh them up."

It did not take long to unload them with three men working on it.

"There, that is the last one," Hudulak said as he placed the last side on the weight scale.

"While you and the butcher work things out, I think I'm going to swing over to the Co-op and pick up some tobacco and rolling papers."

"Sure. I'll meet you back here when you are done."

"You got it, boss man," Hudulak said as he exited the shop.

"Seems like a nice enough fellow," Dackers commented.

"He's a hard worker too, he's never been late, and he never slows down, always looks for things to do. It is going to be tough keeping him busy while I wait to get next year's hogs."

"You can always get him repairing fences," Dackers offered with a smile as he added the last half of the pork. "Well, I have your hog weight all tallied up here. Yes sir, five thousand, eight hundred, and ninety-six pounds, one hundred and four pounds short of six-thousand. That is a good weight Kent. What do you feed them?"

"Organics and a high fiber slop."

"The combination seems to work well," Dackers multiplied the weight by the price he was paying. "At forty-two cents a pound, you've made yourself a pretty penny. Two thousand, four hundred, and seventy-six dollars and some change." Writing out a check in the exact amount, he handed it over. "Here you are. Don't spend it all in one spot," he chuckled.

"No worries there. It goes towards next year's hogs and feed. I might come out on top by five hundred dollars or so. Better than last year and that is a plus in my favor."

"Have you decided how many you'll be raising next year?" Dackers asked. He pulled out a handful of wieners, wrapped them up, and handed them to Kent. "I know how the kids like wieners, so here are a few."

"Thank you. The kids will be smiling tonight. As for next year's hogs, I am thinking an even hundred. It all depends on what the cost is this year."

"Old man Grimes brought in that many this year. His hogs, though, were on the light side." Dackers waved his hand through the air at an annoying fly. "Damn black fly," he muttered. "For as long as I've known Grimes, he's never fed them any special diet, just ordinary slop, and garden waste, I speculate."

"The diet I have my hogs on might cost a bit more, but the results are worth it. That is why old Ed is able to buy that many. His costs are down," Kent responded.

"Yeah, way down. His boys are old enough to work the farm. He doesn't pay them much more than a buck-twenty five an hour." The two of them smiled as Dackers continued. "If his two boys could add, they'd know that their old man is working them too hard for the price he pays them," Dackers shook his head.

"They should've stayed in school. I think his youngest is only fifteen. A kid that age is old enough to work a farm, but I think school is where he should be. I hope my kids are not going to drop out at fifteen. I would like for the three of them to graduate. It makes sense to get a good education in today's world, and then go into the trades," Kent said with hope.

"Speaking of your kids, how are they doing? Sylvia didn't have them with her today."

"No, she dropped them off at the neighbors. Emily, as you know, is in school and loves it. Richard, well, he already wants to buy a butchering hog," he chuckled. "And the youngest is growing like a weed. All in all, I'd say they are as good as can be for their ages."

"That Richard has always been a real go-getter, hasn't he? Are you going to let him get a piglet?"

"I told him that I'd ask him again in a week. I'm not sure I want him to, and then again, I'm not sure I don't. I figured I'd let him decide. I guess my greatest concern is when it comes to butchering. If he gets a piglet, it might become his pet." Kent smiled, "Anyway, looks like my help is here," he said as he spotted Hudulak getting into the truck. "I guess we'll be heading for home. We might make it for dinner yet. Thanks again Dackers, we'll talk soon," Kent said as he waved goodbye.

"Talk to you later Kent. Be careful driving back. I know how that old dirt road can get," Dackers commented as he continued wiping down the counters.

"How did it go, boss man?" Hudulak asked as Kent opened the truck door and sat down.

"Was about one-hundred and forty pounds short of six-thousand, not so bad I figure, did you get what you needed?"

"Sure did. In fact, I think I'm going to have a smoke right now. You don't mind, do you, boss man?"

"Nope, go ahead. I might join you with a pipe full." Kent started the truck, backed up, and honked his horn as he pulled out of Dackers small parking lot. The rain had continued, and as the two of them were about to discover, it had already damaged the road. Three miles outside of Fruitvale where the pavement ended, the road was flooded.

"Holy, look at that, it's a small lake," Kent said as he slowed to a snail's pace. "We better take a look see," he stopped the truck, and they climbed down. "Not sure this old truck can make it through that or not."

"It can't be that deep can it boss man?" Hudulak picked up a rock and tossed it to the middle of the massive puddle. The sound of the *splash* told them that 'yes' it could be that deep.

"There is our answer, I guess." Kent was looking at the obstacle of water. "I think we can get through it if we stick to the high side. The water will not be as deep there. As long as the truck doesn't slip, I think we'll be okay," remembering that behind the truck seat were a set of tire chains, he opened the door, pulled the seat forward and lifted out two sets of chains. He handed a set to Hudulak. "Get those on your side, and I'll do up this side."

"Do you really think chains are necessary, boss man?"

"Not sure, but I'd rather spend a couple of minutes putting chains on than a few hours trying to get unstuck."

"Yeah, I guess that is easier, all right."

It only took a couple of minutes before the task was done. Soaked and cold, they hopped back into the truck.

"Brrrrr, that rain sure is cold."

"Yep, good thing we have heat," Kent said. "It'll warm up in no time. Are you ready to try and cross?"

"Ready as I'll ever be boss man."

With that said, Kent put the truck in gear, and gently stepped on the pedal. The old truck coughed and sputtered as he slowly drove it across the high side of the partially washed-out road. The water was quite high, and some of it sloshed in through the bottom of the doors.

"Whoa, that is deep it soaked my feet."

"Mine too," Kent responded as the truck finally made it to the other side. He tapped his fingers on the dashboard. "Good old girl. Never lets me down," Kent said, with a smile and chuckle.

"Is this a1949 Mercury or 50?" Hudulak asked.

"It's a 1952 actually. It is almost time for a newer one, I think, but I wouldn't dare get one before Sylvia gets her sled," Kent chuckled as he slowed down and turned onto the shoulder. "We'll stop here to take the chains off. No use keeping them on."

"Think they'll have the road fixed up by tomorrow?" Hudulak asked as the two of them stepped out into the downpour.

"It depends on whether they have been notified. If not, I'm sure someone with a tractor, will fix what he can so people can pass. That is what we do around here. We usually have to take care of stuff ourselves."

"I think that is how it is in most farming communities."

"Yep," Kent said as he tossed his chains into the back of the truck. "Toss yours in there when you got them off," he shouted so that Hudulak could hear him above the storm. Opening the door, he slid back into the truck, and rubbed his hands together. It was certainly cold, wet, and miserable. He watched in the mirror as his help tossed his chains into the back of the truck.

"There all done," Hudulak said as he too slid into the cab of the truck. "It sure is coming down now."

There was no doubt about it. It was coming down in droves. It pelted the windshield and the truck cab like someone tapping with a drumstick. It surprised both of them that the wipers continued to work. The blades pushed a quarter inch of water with every pass, it seemed. It gave Kent only about a second to see clearly with each sweeping motion.

"Does it always rain this hard?"

"In the time we've lived here, I've seen it like this maybe half a dozen times. It rains often enough, but not usually this hard and persistent. I think Mother Nature has her seasons mixed up," Kent laughed.

"Usually in October we see frost and hail and maybe a dusting of snow. We don't usually see rain like this."

The two men grew silent as they concentrated on the road in front. The last thing Kent wanted was to go into the ditch. The minutes dragged on. As they crested the last hill before home, they could see Hudu Valley was glowing with sunshine, like an Angel's halo. Whatever storm they were in had dissipated, and Kent pointed it out.

"Look at that. The sun is only now going down in the valley, doesn't look like it rained much here after we left. The dang road is almost dry. The first system must have headed east, and we caught the second one. I hope we make it home before it catches us again." He put the old Mercury into 'Drive' and increased his speed. In his rear view mirror, he could see the dark clouds chasing after them. "It's coming, take a look behind you."

Hudulak turned and looked over his shoulder. The clouds were black as coal and seemed to hover over the small town. "It isn't coming too fast though. Almost looks like it's hanging there in Fruitvale, like it is tied to a string or something."

"It is stuck in the bowl. It will crest that last hill though. I'm betting we'll see it in the valley before dark," Kent signaled off the main highway and onto the road that led them home. The road was a bit muddy, but not as muddy, as it had been when they left. "Looks like the sun came out when we were gone. Pretty much dried everything up now."

"Hopefully, what is coming doesn't show up. That was quite a downpour. Ten times worse than it was here," Hudulak replied as Kent slowed and turned down the road that led to the Townsend farm. They could see that Richard and Emily were outside playing with the dog. "Your kids are home."

"Maybe we've made it in time for dinner," Kent smiled as he rolled down his window. "Hello Emmy, hello Richard. Have you eaten yet?"

"Chicken sandwiches, Dad," Richard called out as Kent pulled into the driveway.

"Did you say chicken sandwiches?" Kent asked as he stepped out of the truck.

"Mom didn't think you and Alex would be home yet. It rained quite hard. Then the sun came out."

"I know we were caught in a storm, ourselves. We even drove through a washout on this side of Fruitvale, just before Marsh Creek."

"Does that mean Emily can stay home tomorrow?"

"It depends I guess. If they don't fix the road, she might have to."

"Hey, Emily," Richard called. "You might have to stay home tomorrow."

"I hope not," she said as she rolled her eyes. "I would be so bored."

"We could find lots to do," Richard responded.

"Like what? Put worms on a hook?" Emily said, with sarcasm and disdain. Missing one day of school was the worst thing that could happen. She loved to learn.

"We're not going to worry about it until tomorrow Emmy. For the time being, if the road is fixed, you'll be at school tomorrow. The sooner I phone the Highway Department, the sooner they might fix it," Kent said as he rubbed Richard's head, and made his way to the house.

Hudulak stayed behind and leaned against the truck as he rolled a cigarette. He was watching Emily as she bounced on her pogo stick. "How many is that?" he asked as he brought a match to the cigarette dangling from his mouth.

"I wasn't counting."

"I have a quarter that says you can't jump on that thing fifty times." He inhaled a lung full of smoke, "What do you say?"

As Emily looked at him, her stomach, for one reason or another, told her not to take him up on the offer; that his intent was malicious. He made her uncomfortable. She had a sixth sense that something was not right about him. "You are probably right. I couldn't do it fifty times," she jumped off and leaned it against the house.

"You'll never know unless you try."

"I don't want to."

"All right," he shrugged his shoulders, turned, and looked toward the barn. Richard and Emily continued to play. Every now and again he would look back at them intently, his eyes on Emily. Sylvia opened the front door and called the kids to come in and get ready for their baths.

"Please, a few more minutes, Mom!" Richard yelled back. "Emmy and I are playing a spelling game. Every time one of us drops the ball, we have to spell a word."

"Another twenty minutes only, okay?" Sylvia, seeing that Hudulak was standing by the truck, waved her hand in a friendly gesture. With a smile, he waved back.

"Hello, boss lady."

"There is some chicken left. Are you hungry, Alex?"

"Nah, maybe I'll have some toast, later. I'm good."

"Okay," Sylvia closed the door, and went to the dining room table to sit with Kent, who was trying to reach the Highways Department.

"Nothing yet?" she asked.

Kent shook his head. "No one is answering. Maybe someone else got through. What time is it?"

"It is a little after six o'clock, everyone there has probably gone home for the day."

"I would imagine, I'll make it to work tomorrow, but Emmy might have to stay home if the bus is not running. I don't know how it will get past that washout. Hopefully, it will get fixed overnight." Kent shrugged his shoulders indicating how unlikely that was. The real hope, of course, was that one of the farmers near the area would use his tractor to patch it up.

Even a temporary fix would make it better. It could be that one of the culverts plugged up or ripped away. If that were the case, the road to town would not be passable for a few days, and there would be a detour set up through a farmer's field. That had happened once before, near the same place where the washout was. Pulling out his pipe, he filled the bowl.

"I guess now is a good time to go through our finances. The butcher paid us pretty good this time."

"What did all the hogs weigh?" asked Sylvia.

"All together it was five thousand-eight hundred and ninety six pounds. Not bad, we were so close to six thousand. Anyway, the check he wrote out is for two-thousand-four hundred and seventy six dollars and thirty-two cents. He paid us forty-two cents a pound. It is a bit more than I expected."

"That is pretty good. Hypothetically, that is more than a year of mortgage payments."

"That is true, but that is not where it is going," he said as he kissed her on the cheek. "I have to catch up on my feed bill, and arrange for more piglets. Some has to go into our savings, and the kids need some new clothes and shoes. We also have to consider Christmas which is fast approaching."

Kent took a long pull on his pipe and smiled. "We have a lot to come out, but I think we will do okay this Christmas. We'll even be able to get Emily that doll she wants. She does still want it, doesn't she?" he asked.

"As far as I know she does. You have to remember that was what she wanted last year."

"I know. I wish we could have gotten it for her then." Falling silent, he thought about the things the kids wanted. They always seemed to be things that were unaffordable at the time. This year though, things were different. Years of struggling, budgeting, and hard work were beginning to make a difference. "Whether she wants it this year or not, I say we buy it for her along with what she might want this year. Same with Richard and Jack, whatever we couldn't get them last year let's get for them this year. They deserve a special Christmas. This year we are sitting all right, and we can do it."

"Let's not get too far ahead of ourselves. As you said, you have to pay down the feed bill, and buy next year's hogs," Sylvia said.

"True enough. We'll straighten all that out before we go shopping." Kent looked out the kitchen window contemplating. He desired nothing more than giving his children all that they wanted.

In reality, that was not always possible. It tugged at his heartstrings. Sylvia and Kent's children were their world. Everything they did was for them. That was one reason they had bought their little piece of paradise. The security of owning a farm benefitted the kids. They did not have to grow up in a concrete jungle. There were fields they could walk, creeks they could fish or swim in, and a large parcel of land they could call their own. It was true that there was always work to do on a farm, but it was better than having nothing to do. A large city lot did not compare to acres of land. He was content with the decision to buy the farm, for there was, without a doubt, no better place for their children to grow.

The porch door opened, and they could hear the children as they made their way into the kitchen, teasing each other.

"You didn't spell it right, Richard."

"Did too."

"Did not."

"Let's ask mom?"

"Fine."

"Ask mom what?" Sylvia interjected.

"How to spell porcupine," Emily said.

"That is a tough word. You didn't expect Richard to spell that did you?"

"I can spell it Mom; it is P O R Q U P I N E."

"That is how it sounds, but not how it is spelled."

"See, told you Richard."

"Whatever, Emmy," Richard said as he stuck out his tongue.

"All right you two that is enough. Can you spell it, Emmy?" Sylvia asked.

"P O R C U P I N E," Emily put her hands on her hips. "That is how it is spelled."

"That is right, but, Richard was close. All he had to do was to replace the Q with a C."

"So, it is P O R C U P I N E?" Richard wanted to be sure.

"Yes."

"Now I know how to spell it. You were right Emmy. Sorry I made you mad," Richard said.

"That's okay. It was still fun. I won't ask you to spell such difficult words the next time we play."

"Can we play again tomorrow?"

"Maybe," Emily said as she made her way into the dining room. "Hello, Daddy."

"Hello darling."

"Did you call the road people?"

"I did sweetheart, but no one was there."

"Does that mean I will have to stay home tomorrow?"

Kent tried to appease her. "Even if you did it wouldn't be so bad would it?"

"I don't know. I could do work in my phonics book, I guess."

"Or you could take the day off and help your mom with Jack and Richard. It wouldn't hurt you to stay away from books for a day."

"If I do stay home, I will do some phonics in the morning, and then I'll help mom."

89

"We will know in the morning if the bus is going to come. Maybe one of the farmers will have fixed the road by then." Kent smiled at her and winked.

"I'm going to go have my bath now."

"Yep, you go ahead sweetie," Kent replied as he watched her scurry off.

"Don't use all the hot water though. Jack and Richard need baths too."

"I know," Emily called back.

By 8:00 o'clock that evening, the children were finished with their baths, and a half-hour later, were all tucked away in their beds, they were sleeping soundly.

"Well, the last few days turned out pretty good except for the rain," Kent began as he, Sylvia, and Hudulak sat at the table drinking the last of their coffee. "Sure hope the road gets fixed. Emily is not going to be happy if she has to stay home. That girl can't get enough of learning."

"Nothing wrong with that, boss man. She's a smart kid, and smart kids want to learn. It is like they absorb everything, kind of like a sponge." Hudulak took a swig from his coffee. "Is it all right if I smoke?" he asked.

"I didn't know you smoked, Alex," Sylvia stated.

"I do once in a while. I haven't picked any tobacco up until today though."

"Sure, go ahead and smoke. I'll join you with a pipe," Kent said. "But, please, don't smoke in your bedroom. I don't want Jack and Richard getting sick."

"No. I'd never smoke in there, boss man." Hudulak rolled a cigarette and inhaled deeply. "That feels good," he said as he exhaled. The room was silent for a few minutes as Kent and Hudulak smoked, and Sylvia sipped her tea.

"I guess you folks did well in the hog harvesting this year, eh?" Hudulak brought up.

"We did, yep. Next year we'll even do better especially since I will have you helping," Kent nodded his appreciation.

"Thanks, boss man. I'm not used to getting compliments like that."

"If you deserve compliments, you should get them," Sylvia stated.

"And if you don't, you won't," Kent added, with a smile.

"That makes perfect sense," Hudulak said as he butted out his cigarette. "Well folks, I'm off to bed. See you in the morning."

Chapter 10

Hudulak woke the next day before the others. It was Tuesday, October 21, 1958. The sound of thunder woke him. It was strange that no one else even budged. He made his way to the kitchen and turned on the coffee pot. It was 4:45 a.m., and Kent would not be up for a few more minutes. Hudulak took the opportunity to roll a cigarette and sit alone at the table, a coffee in hand.

Looks like a crappy one today, he thought as he puffed on the cigarette. He turned the volume knob on the radio down, and then turned it on. The 6:00 o'clock news would not be on for another hour, but the quiet music woke him up a bit. He yawned and stretched. *I wonder what the boss man is going to have me do today.* He sipped his coffee, *can't do much outside in weather like this.* His mind drifted as he sat there and finished his first coffee. He was about to get up and pour his second when Kent came in.

"Good morning Alex."

"Morning boss man, can you believe it? It is still raining cats and dogs outside."

"I see that. I would appreciate the rain if it were spring. Don't have much use for it in the fall."

"No kidding," Hudulak rolled another cigarette while Kent poured himself a coffee. "It doesn't give a man much choice on what to do."

"You got that right. I think today is a good day to stay inside. I know the barn and hayloft need some maintenance. You could spend some time fixing the odd broken board. The hayloft ladder needs some work. A couple of the rungs should be replaced."

"True enough. I could also count the hog slop and straw bales we have."

"Good idea, yeah, that will be fine. If the rain slows or stops, you could get started on building the new pigpen outside. That would be good. We have to beat Mother Nature and do it before the ground freezes. It should be about twenty foot by twenty foot. A good place I think would be right under that old poplar tree that sits on the hill. It'll give the hogs shade from the sun and keep them dry from the rain."

"Sure, I know the spot you are talking about. It's likely going to be rocky digging in that dirt."

"We have picks and shovels. To start it off, we are going to need the corner posts in first so we can line it all up."

"If I can get to it today, I'll measure it all out. It might be a good idea to build the pen around the tree. If the tree isn't in the middle or close to it, climbing predators like cougar, maybe even a bear, might climb right in. That'd be a mess. Are there cougars around here, boss man?"

"A few folks have seen them, but I haven't. There are many cinnamon and black bears, though. We see them every spring in the fields around here. You make a good point Alex. The pen should be built around the tree, far enough from the rails that nothing will be able to climb it. We'll have to go up the hill a bit further than I wanted, but that is okay." Kent sipped from his coffee. "If we have to, we'll use the small pen for the misfits."

Hudulak looked at him, "Misfits, what do you mean?" he asked with some confusion on what exactly Kent meant.

"Sometimes hogs will fight each other, we'll have to put those ones separate from the rest. That small corral will do for that."

"Oh, okay, I see. I wasn't sure what you meant by misfits. I get it now. I didn't know that about hogs."

"They can be pretty nasty to each other. Once they get a taste for it, it is hard to break them from the habit." The timer on the stove buzzed telling Kent his boiled eggs were ready. "Have you had breakfast yet?" he asked Hudulak.

"Nope, I've only had a coffee so far."

"I boiled a half dozen of eggs you are welcome to share if you are hungry."

"That's okay, boss man. Coffee will do for now. I'll eat a big lunch."

"All right," Kent put the eggs in a bowl and bread in the toaster. A few minutes later, he sat down with his eggs and toast in front of him. "I guess Emily will be staying home today since we're not sure the road is open. She isn't going to be happy about that," Kent chuckled.

"I'm sure Richard and Jack will keep her on her toes," Hudulak replied as he puffed on his second cigarette.

"I'm sure they will keep her amused if nothing else. She and Richard might get under foot. Watch out for that."

"I'll put them to work. I could find something fun and easy for them to do if they get bored."

"Feel free. I'm sure Richard wouldn't mind. Emily, on the other hand, might," Kent smiled.

"She likes to count stuff so I could have her count the bags of hog slop we have left."

Kent nodded. "That might be something you'll be able to get her to do," he responded as he ate the last of his breakfast. "Well, it's almost 5:45. I guess I should head out. I hope that washout is not any worse. With the rain, we've had, I can almost bet that it is. You might see me back here before you know it." Kent stood from the table and set his dishes in the sink. "I'll see you later Alex."

"You bet, boss man. Have a good day." Hudulak rose from the table making his way into the kitchen, where he poured his third coffee of the morning. Sitting back down he waited for the 6:00 a.m., news to come on. He listened for the first few minutes, and then headed to the barn to see what he could start doing. He never liked being in the house when everyone else woke. It was always so noisy and chaotic. He always wanted to be down at the barn by then.

The rain slowed to a trickle, but everything was wet and miserable. He lit the boiler to warm the place up. It was strange being in the barn without a bunch of squealing hogs. The only sound was an audible 'drip, drip' that seemed to be coming from the stalls. Walking down the corridor to the back door, he noticed where the roof had sprung a few leaks. *I guess I best look at that later. Maybe boss man has a pail of tar somewhere I hope,* he thought as he slid open the back door. The sun was trying to peek through the clouds. *Looks like it'll lighten up today after all. Good. Some sunshine will dry everything up.*

He leaned against the sliding door frame and rolled a cigarette. Taking in the little sun there was and knowing that soon enough snow would be upon them, he took his time to smoke. He remembered that there were a couple of old coffee cups and a kettle down by the boiler, so he made his way there. The instant coffee and the old sugar were good enough for him once he wiped the ants away from the cubes. He rinsed the kettle out, filled it with fresh water, and set it on the top of the boiler. While he waited for the water to boil, he added more logs trying to warm the barn to a comfortable temperature and remove some of the dampness. He was not sure which task to start first. Perhaps the coffee would help him decide.

He sat on one of the sawhorses and leisurely sipped from the cup in his hands. Content as he was, he still battled a feeling of uselessness. *I shouldn't be sitting on my ass. There is work to do,* he thought as he set his cup down.

All his life, he had the feeling of being useless if he were not actively doing something. That was thanks to his mother who was always nagging him to do work for her. His childhood had not been normal. He seldom played with other kids. He had to work, work, work, from the time he was old enough to do so. On those rare occasions when he did take a day off, his mother would yell at him, saying he was lazy, and called him names.

He opened the tool crib door where Kent kept everything. He hoped to find a tub of tar. He did find a tape measure, some wooden stakes, and a roll of string, but no tar. "That's a good find. I can measure the hog pen boss man wants to build," he said beneath his breath as he looked for something to hold the tools. An empty five-gallon bucket would do. "I know I saw an old hammer somewhere. Ah, there it is." He put the string, tape measure, wooden stakes, and hammer, into the empty bucket. *That'll keep me busy for a half hour or so. Might even get a couple of the corner posts dug, depending if the ground isn't as hard as pavement,* he thought.

Exiting the barn with the bucket of tools, he climbed over the fence snagging his shirtsleeve. The bucket fell to the ground spilling the tools. "Damn it!" he said aloud as he untangled the wire. Picking up the bucket and tools, he walked to the old poplar tree. It was plush with autumn colors, almost brilliant in its luxurious reds and yellows.

Leafs fell from it as a mild breeze picked up. They skimmed across all the other dead and dry leafs, making a crackling noise. For a brief moment, he was in awe of the dazzling colors. He turned to look at the surrounding bush line and realized that he hadn't paid much attention to the changing colors. *Things we take for granted,* he thought as he set the bucket down.

The first two stakes that he lined up sank into the ground with ease. The third and fourth gave him trouble. The ground where they needed to be was annoyingly hard and rocky. He finally gave up and moved over a few feet. *A couple of extra feet isn't going to make a difference, I don't suppose,* he thought, as he sat down on a large rock that protruded near where the middle of where the pen would be.

After a few minutes of contemplation and thought, he hammered the last two stakes into the ground, and tied off the string to keep things straight and to get a visual on how the pen might look.

It was a fair size, and as square as he could get it. He liked things symmetrical. Anything else always made him feel as though he were in a whirlwind of chaos. He did not know why he felt that way, but when things were not in their place, or things were out of alignment, he always felt anxiety and confusion. It had been that way his entire life. He reminisced as he sat in the silence of the moment thinking. The late morning sun appeared and warmed his face as the mild breeze picked up once more. Rested, he rose from the ground, gathered the tools he used, and returned to the barn. He set the bucket on the floor of the tool crib, and leaned the shovel and pick against the wall. He liked the way Kent kept things. Everything was, organized, in a planned fashion. It was how he would want things to be on a farm.

Closing the tool crib door, he swung the pick and shovel over his shoulder. Ready to start digging holes, Hudulak headed back to the poplar tree. He started with the holes on the top side to keep the warm sun in his face.

He was surprised at how hot it did get. By mid-day, there was no sign of the two-day storm that hit the region. It was as warm as a late spring day. He took his time with the last hole he was digging, resting whenever he felt the need. Finally, with a last scoop of dirt, all four corner post-holes were finished.

Hudulak sighed, *time for a cigarette,* he thought as he looked at his work. It had not been all that, difficult. Still, there were the holes to dig for the posts that would have to go between the corner posts. Shrugging his shoulders, he waved his hand through the air. *Ah, it is just work,* he thought as he inhaled a deep lung-full of smoke.

Hearing his name called, he looked toward the barn he could see Sylvia and the kids wandering around looking for him.

"Over here!" he yelled as he made his way down the slope.

"Oh, there you are," Sylvia said as she spotted him.

"I was getting the corner posts dug for the pen boss man wants to build."

"Is the digging hard, Alex?" Richard asked.

"Some places are, but, nah, it has been pretty easy so far. What brings you folks down here?"

"I was hoping you could keep an eye on Richard and Emily. I have to deliver some eggs, out toward Salmo, and they don't want to come. It is only for a half hour. I'll be taking Jack with me."

Hudulak saw no problem with that. "Boss man and I talked about that this morning. If the two of them want to help me, I have a few things they could do." He made his way closer to where they were standing. "Emmy could count out how many sacks of hog feed we have left, and Richard can help her or start with cleaning the rabbit pens. There are also today's eggs to gather."

"Actually, I already got those," Sylvia said. "Thanks so much, Alex. I'll be back before you know it. Come on, Jack, let's go." She took Jack by the hand who insisted that he walk. "See you guys later."

"Yeah, later, boss lady. All right you two. I'll show you what you can help with. C'mon."

"I know where the feed is. You don't have to show me," Emily stated.

"I know that, but there are two kinds. Don't argue."

"Whatever." Emily followed behind wishing that she were in school or, at the least, wishing now that she had gone with her mother. Hudulak opened the hay barn door and waited for Emily and Richard to enter. They made their way over to the two stacks of feed.

"Okay. This one is the high fiber stuff your dad has been feeding the hogs, and this stack is what he uses to start the piglets off, there is no need to move any of it. You can pretty much count them by doing your math. You know, count how many there are across and multiply by how many there are up and down."

"I know how to do that. It's called a mathematical formula," Emily replied.

"Good," Hudulak said as he snatched a clipboard off the wall that was, used to keep track of supplies. "You can use this to write down the amounts," he handed Emily the clipboard. "I'll check back with you in a few minutes after I clean up the tools I used this morning." He didn't like Emily's attitude and he felt like slapping her. Instead, he walked out and went about cleaning up the tools.

He covered up the holes with boards to keep debris out and to keep any wandering animals from breaking their legs. The rest of the holes he would finish another day. He knew that the timbers and lumber hadn't been ordered yet, which meant he was ahead of the game.

"That'll please boss man I think," he said quietly as he looked back at his work. The pen was not the size they discussed. Rather than being 20x20, it was 24x20. *I guess I'll know for sure if it makes him happy when he sees it.* Hudulak ran his hand across his chin in deep contemplation. *I'm not sure a pen that size is big enough. Ah, I'll let boss man decide.*

He headed back to the barn to put the shovel and pick away. Stopping briefly at the water hose, he took a long drink. His stomach was telling him that it was past lunch. He wasn't sure though what time it was, he didn't own a watch. For now, time was just that... time. Traipsing across the barnyard to the hay barn, he checked in on Emily and Richard. "Do you kids know what time it might be?"

"When we came down here it was almost 11:00 o'clock," Emily said.

"That's all?" Hudulak asked in disbelief.

"It was something like that, Alex."

"Humph, all right then. How is the counting coming, Emily? Are you almost done?"

"I was done a long time ago. I wrote it all down," she handed Hudulak the clipboard.

"Thanks." He took it from her and looked at it briefly then hung it back on the wall. "So, there are twenty-two high fiber sacks and thirty-six of the pig starter?"

"That is what I counted."

"Well done, Emily, what about the rabbit cage? Did you get it cleaned out Richard?"

"We haven't even started that Alex. We were talking."

"Oh, about what?" he pried.

"It was nothing really, just talking," Emily responded.

The truth was they had been talking about him. Emily was telling Richard how truly creepy she thought he was. Richard realized it was true that Alex acted strangely around Emily and even around his mother sometimes. Maybe Emily did have a reason to feel that way.

"Okay," Hudulak, nodded, he wasn't stupid. "The rabbits can't clean their cage themselves."

"Yeah, Emmy, Alex is right, let's get the cage cleaned."

"Fine," Emily said as she moved closer to Richard and the door that led to the rabbit cage. "We should probably get them fresh water and feed too," she said as she opened the door.

Hudulak watched as the door closed behind them. *That girl is a bit too smart for her own good,* his mind raced. He needed something to do, to get away from Emily. He would not be able to control the monster inside himself if he let her get in his mind. *Now isn't the time,* he thought.

Emily was looking out the window watching him as he slipped into the hog barn. "There he is in the other barn now. He creeps me out Richard."

"Don't worry about it, Emmy. You don't know him as well as I do. I know he acts funny around you and mom, but I don't think he knows any better. He is from way up North. Might have even lived in an igloo," Richard laughed, trying to break the tension as he opened the rabbit cage and began cleaning it.

"You are silly Richard. He lived on a farm like ours, so he lived in a house."

"Yeah, but it was still way up North."

"It doesn't matter where you come from Richard. People are people," she pointed toward the other barn. "He seems a little strange to me. I guess you are right though. I haven't been around him as much as you and Jack so I can't even say that. Daddy always says first impressions are either good or bad. My first impression is 'bad'. I think he is a creep."

"Maybe after you know him some more you won't feel that way."

"I doubt that," Emily stated as she too began cleaning the cage. It didn't take long, and before they knew it, the cage was cleaned, and the rabbits were fed and watered. "There, all done," Emily, said with relief. "Mom should be home soon. Do you want to play 'Drop the Ball, Spell a Word'?"

"Okay, but no hard words. I can't spell those very well."

"How else are you going to get good at spelling if you don't try to spell big words?"

"When I go to school I guess." Richard shrugged his shoulders as he and Emily left the barn. The sound of the barnyard gate opening caught Hudulak's attention. He was hoping it was Sylvia. He looked through the barn window and saw only Emily and Richard. *I wonder what they're doing,* he thought as he made his way to the door.

"Hey you kids! What are you doing now?" he yelled out.

"We're going to go play up at the house. Is that okay Alex?" Richard called back.

"Did you get the rabbit cage clean?"

"Yep."

"I don't know if your mom wants you guys up at the house. Can't you play down here where I can keep my eye on you? I'd get in a lot of trouble from your dad if either of you got hurt on my watch."

"We'll be careful," Emily tried to convince him.

"Stay in sight, okay?" Hudulak was not sure if he should let them go or not, but in all honestly he didn't care; he wasn't a babysitter.

"Yep, we'll be playing on the grass."

"All right then, as long as I can see you from down here. I don't want to be looking for you."

"Thanks Alex," Richard waved as he closed the gate and followed Emily.

Hudulak watched the two children hop and skip back to the house. He finally looked in the right place in the barn and found a half-empty five-gallon bucket of tar. He opened it and tried to stir it to a consistency for spreading, but it was too hard. Instead, he set it near the boiler, and although the barn was warm, he added another armful of wood. It would not take long for the tar to soften, and when it finally did, he would set up a ladder and patch the leaks in the roof. That would keep him busy until the end of the day.

His next order of business was to find something to spread the tar. An old paintbrush or putty knife would work. He found neither. *Damn it, I guess I'll use a piece of wood,* he thought as he wandered outside to the back of the barn. He found a suitable piece of wood, and used the pig-sticking knife to carve it into a paddle shape.

"There, that'll work." He looked at the paddle in his hand. *Could use this to smack her on her ass,* he thought. He did not know whom he was thinking about, but women in general would suffice. He slapped it against the palm of his hand. "That'd put a sting on her ass," he chuckled as he checked on the bucket of tar. *Ready as it will ever be, I suppose,* he thought as he stirred it until it was, mixed thoroughly. He leaned the ladder against the side of the roof of the hog barn.

With tar bucket in hand, he climbed up and made his way to the place where he calculated the leaks to be. Sure enough, there were a few places where the metal roof had rusted through. He spread some tar on the holes and walked the length of the roof checking for more holes. He patched them as he found them. The smell of the tar in the hot sun made him feel lightheaded. In the distance, Sylvia's car approached.

"Good. Maybe I can get some lunch." In hindsight, he wished he had taken Kent's offer to join him in eggs and toast that morning. He waited until Sylvia was in the driveway before he climbed off the roof and headed toward the house. "How did the egg selling go today, boss lady?" he asked.

"Sold them all, the road out to Salmo is sure in rough shape. Sorry it took so long." Sylvia set Jack down, and he ran toward Richard and Emily. "Slow down, Jack. Be careful. He's a tyrant today," Sylvia said as she sighed. "I'll get your lunch ready right away Alex. Is soup and grilled-cheese sandwiches okay?"

"Yeah, that would be perfect. I am hungry. Thanks, boss lady."

"No problem. Do you want to come in now? I can warm up the coffee."

"Are the kids going to be all right?" he asked, as though he cared.

"Yes, they'll watch Jack. He'll be okay," she responded.

"All right, I could use a coffee. The smell of the tar I'm putting on the roof makes me feel woozy." He followed Sylvia into the house watching her from behind closely. Even in her farm clothes, she was dreamy.

"You are tarring a roof?" Sylvia asked.

"Yeah, I noticed the hog barn was leaking this morning. I'll get her all fixed up today though," Hudulak said as he sat down on the porch bench and removed his boots. "Turned out to be a pretty nice day today, eh, boss lady?"

"We know better than to get used to it though. It always changes. I don't think we've had storms like this past couple of days in a year or so. With Halloween being only a week away, the weather is going to get cold. It might even snow. It always seems to on Halloween."

"I guess we better enjoy the sunshine while we can."

"Yes," Sylvia said as she stepped into the kitchen and turned the coffee on. "The coffee will be ready in a few minutes. I'll get the soup and sandwiches started."

Hudulak nodded as he stepped past her. "That will be great," he said. He headed to the bathroom to wash his hands.

"Can you eat one or two grilled cheese, Alex?"

"Two will do the job, thanks. I should have had breakfast this morning, but I wasn't hungry then. Am now though," he chuckled as he turned on the bathroom sink and washed his hands.

"Breakfast is the most important meal of the day," Sylvia replied, loud enough for him to hear as she stirred the soup and flipped the grilled cheese.

"I know. Just wasn't hungry. Not sure why." Hudulak dried his hands then made his way to the dining room table.

"Maybe you were tired of eating eggs. You could have eaten other things. We have hot or cold cereal, toast, that type of thing."

"I suppose. I never thought of it. A couple of grilled cheese sandwiches and a bowl or two of soup and I'll be good to go." He was watching her, with her back turned, his view was good. Hudulak's only thought, at that moment, wasn't on food. He was conjuring up a fantasy and Sylvia was the star. He sat silently, his mind racing with thoughts of her. So intense was the fantasy dancing in his head that his heart sped up. He was quick to avert his eyes from her backside the moment she turned toward him.

"All done, come and get it," Sylvia said as she pulled out a few small plates and bowls.

Hudulak rose from the table and gathered his lunch. "It sure smells good. Is there ketchup? I like ketchup with my grilled cheese."

"It's in the fridge. Help yourself, Alex. I'm going to call the kids in." Sylvia stepped into the porch and opened the front door. "Emily, Richard, Jack! Lunch is ready! Come and get it while it is hot," she called out to them.

"Coming Mom, we'll be right there," Emily replied.

"Okay sweetie." Sylvia closed the front door and stepped back into the kitchen. She cut Emily and Richard's, grilled cheese sandwich in half and ladled out a bowl of soup for each of them, as the kids came dashing in.

"All right you three. Go wash up. I'll put your lunch on the table." Sylvia weaved in between the children as they ran to the bathroom to clean up. "Whoa you guys, slow down. I almost spilled your soup."

"Sorry Mom, but we're in a real hurry. Jack is playing catch with us and caught the ball three times in a row," Richard replied with pride for his little brother. "He's a real good catcher."

"That is fine, but we don't run in the house, especially when we are about to eat. That could be dangerous," Sylvia replied sternly, but with a smile.

"Okay," Richard replied as he darted to the bathroom.

Sylvia shook her head. "They're little tyrants today the lot of them."

Hudulak smiled as she set down the kids' lunches. "They're just having fun," he slurped the last of his soup. "That was darned good, boss lady. Thank you for it." He was eating his second sandwich when the kids sat down. He nodded at them. "Tell us again Richard, how many times did Jack catch the ball? Did I hear three times?"

"Yeah, in a row," Richard said, with his eyes big as he crumbled crackers into his bowl of soup.

"Three times eh? That is pretty good for a little fellow isn't it?"

"He never caught a ball that many times before. Not in a row anyway," Emily added.

Hudulak looked over to Jack. "Is that right, Jack? You've never caught the ball three times in a row before?" he questioned with fun in his voice as though Jack would give him an answer. "That's all right, little fellow. You practice up with Emmy and Richard, and before you know it, you'll be catching that ball every time." He smiled and rose from the table. "Anyway, I have to get back to the barn. Thank you again, boss lady. It was real good," Hudulak put his bowl and plate in the sink.

"You are very welcome, Alex."

He nodded then stepped into the porch. Sitting on the bench, he slipped on his boots, rolled a cigarette, and headed back to the barn. His stomach was satisfied, and he felt good. *"Boy, that woman can cook,"* he thought as he opened the barnyard gate.

He decided to walk over to the creek and check on the fences in that area. There were a couple of loose strands of barbed wire and seven broken posts. *Looks like I got my work cut out for tomorrow. No use starting now, boss man is going to be home soon,* he thought as he climbed over the fence and took a long cold drink from the creek. He rose and wiped his chin. Following the fence a little further, he checked posts and the wire. Looking around he heard the flapping of a grouse as it passed a few feet from him. It landed clumsily then vanished into the undergrowth. *Should have had boss man's .22 rifle that was a nice plump one.*

Taking his time now, he ambled back to the barn and over to a stack of fence posts. He dug out seven of the better ones and stacked them neatly for easy access. *There, all ready for the morning.*

After dinner, that evening, Hudulak showed Kent the work he did, for the new hog pen. "It is a little bigger than you wanted, but I'm not sure it is large enough for a hundred hogs. Maybe when they are little, but not when they mature," Hudulak said, as the two of them arrived.

106

Kent took his pipe out of his shirt pocket and filled it with tobacco. "It does look small, doesn't it? That is okay though because we won't have all one hundred in there at one time. We'll rotate them every day, twenty today, twenty tomorrow, that type of thing."

"I think, even for only twenty a day, a bigger size would be better. We should go thirty-foot by thirty-foot, maybe."

"That would be a better size, now that I'm looking at it." Kent grew silent for a moment as he contemplated. "Okay, we'll make it that size. How long do you think it'll take to finish the holes?"

"There are a few posts needing replacement on the fence by the creek. I'll finish with that fence first. I could have these holes here dug by the weekend."

"All right, so I'll order the timbers and planks tomorrow. How many do you think we'll need?"

"I'd say at least forty, fifteen-footers. A couple extra wouldn't hurt. It's always better to have a few more than not enough."

"I'll order enough. Also, we'll need at least ten or so timbers for the posts." Kent took a long pull on his pipe and exhaled. "Sylvia mentioned that you patched the hog barn roof too. I do that every year. I think what it needs is new metal. That won't be for another year or so. That stuff is expensive." He was quite pleased with the work his help did that day. "I'd say you put in a good day's work today." It was hard for him to offer compliments, but if a person deserved them, then he would offer them.

"Thank you, boss man. I'm glad you are pleased."

Kent nodded. "I am, let's head back to the house. The News will be on soon."

"Right behind you," Hudulak responded as the two of them made their way back to the house. "I think we should build a hog run from the barn to the pen, it'll make it easier to put them outside and to bring them back in."

"That is a good idea. Make it so it is at least ten feet from the back door. We can use temporary rails when we move them in and out. The run should be probably six to eight foot wide, with a gate at both ends."

"That sounds about right. You're going to need to order a few more planks though."

"That's all right. We'll order them when the posts are in the ground, for the run, we can use ordinary fence posts for that. I have a stack already."

"I saw that. That is where I pulled out the seven posts I need for that fence by the creek. There are enough of those for sure."

"I'd say you have your work cut out for you until the end of the week at least."

"I'm never worried about finding stuff to do. There is always something I can find to work on."

"Have you used a chainsaw before?"

"I have, yep."

"Good because there are a few things we need done. I'll show you the cedar tree I want to fall. We will use it for making fence posts. Cedar seems to be the best. It doesn't rot as quickly."

"You must use wedges and splitting mauls to make posts, I bet," Hudulak commented.

"Those and a bit of muscle," Kent chuckled. "I usually fall a cedar tree once a year to let the posts get seasoned before planting them in the ground. Since we will be using some from the stack I already have, we'll need to replenish the pile for next year. Might need more posts because I'm thinking of running another fence along the road, in case I pick up a couple of dairy cows next fall."

"I have to tell you, boss man that I have never milked a cow."

Kent smiled. "There is nothing to it. Besides, I'm not getting them right away. It is something though that I've been thinking about."

By week's end, Hudulak managed to finish the work. The post holes for the pen were dug out and ready, and the posts were in place for the hog run that ran from barn to the outside pen. All he needed now were the planks and timbers. It was the 24 of October and luckily, the weather remained decent, which made it easier for him to get all the work finished. He had the weekend now to relax.

Chapter 11

Three days later the weather turned and brought with it an early morning frost. It seemed odd how it changed so quickly. A deep, white frost covered the ground, it almost looked as though it had snowed. It burned off though as the yellow sun rose.

"Good thing you got all the post holes dug. The ground is going to start to freeze up soon," Kent said as Hudulak sat down with his morning coffee.

"I was thinking the same thing. It sure did get cold."

"By mid-morning the sun will warm things up. I expect we'll have snow by the end of the week."

"As long as we have the timbers for the pen in place, it can snow all it wants."

"The timbers and the lumber will likely be delivered by mid-week. That will give us a day or two to get them in the ground," Kent responded as he went back to his eggs and toast. "That reminds me, we also have to get the hog stalls painted. I paint them every year before I get new stock. It keeps the mites and fleas at bay."

"Is there paint? If there is paint I could start that today," Hudulak took a drink from his coffee.

Kent chewed for a moment as he tried to remember if there was or not, "I believe that there is, it's in the top part of the tool crib. You have to use the ladder, but it should be within reach once you open the little door. There should be a little more than five gallons of each, floor paint and wall paint, or at least enough to get started. If we need more, I will pick that up later in the week on my way home. The white color is for the walls, the concrete ones, and the wood. The grey is for the floors. You have to put it on thick. Start with painting the insides first. The outside, and corridor can be done anytime. Get the boiler going and turn on the big fan. It will blow enough heat to warm it up so the paint will adhere. Otherwise, it will be a mess. I know from experience."

"Guess I got my work cut out for me today, I kind of enjoy painting. It's a good change for a day."

"Avoid inhaling the fumes. It is strong smelling paint and can make you quite dizzy. Painting does two things, it cleans everything up and prevents the mites and other nuisances from laying eggs. The last thing we want is a hog mite infestation. The mange they cause can get costly." Kent looked at his watch. "Well, it's time for me to head out. I'll see you later Alex," he rose from the table, and as he did every morning, he set his dishes in the sink.

"Yep, I'll see you later, boss man. I'll get the painting started. Might even get most of it finished if there is enough paint."

"Good enough." Kent stepped into the porch, sat at the bench, and put his boots on. With a heavy sigh, he headed out into the frozen morning.

Hudulak sat at the table and watched as the trucks taillights vanished. Rolling a cigarette, he inhaled deeply, and then slowly slurped his coffee. Who was he, kidding? He hated painting. It was one of the worst things to do. *Paint, they're just hogs for Christ sake. Mite's, who gives a shit,* he thought as he exhaled. *Oh well, pay day this Friday. I think I'll get myself a ride into town and spend Friday night at the hotel, and maybe get myself a little momma to play with. I'm getting tired of this shit already.*

When the sun rose, and the frost-covered ground sparkled with dew, Hudulak dressed in an old pair of corduroy pants and went to the barn. He tossed a couple of dry pieces of wood onto the remnants of a few coals, and the fire took to life. *There that'll get things warmed up,* he thought as he leaned a stepladder against the tool crib wall.

"I should be able to reach from there, I suppose," he said, quietly. He stepped up and opened the small door at the top. Sure enough, inside within his reach were two five-gallon buckets of paint, grey and white. He took the first one down and set it near the boiler. The second was a bit heavier than he expected, and he almost fell.

"Damn it! Whoa, that was a little too close for comfort. Would have hated to clean up a mess of paint," he said as he caught his balance and stepped down.

Two hours later, he was slapping on paint. He started with the walls and decided to paint all of them before committing to the floors. The floors would be easier to paint. Luckily, he had found an old cornhusk broom, the handle broken at midpoint. He affixed a piece of wood to the handle, making it a bit longer.

His plan was clear he would finish with the walls, and then use the old broom to paint the floors. It was wider than, a paintbrush and better than a roller and would make the job go faster. It would also lay the paint down nice and thick. By lunch, he managed to paint three of the sixteen stalls.

Making his way down the barn corridor, he heard Sylvia call his name. "Alex, I have your lunch," she called out to him.

"Right here, boss lady," he said as he made his way to her.

"I hope you don't mind that it is just some sandwiches and a few baked goods plus a thermos of coffee. I have to go deliver eggs again, but Richard and Jack are coming with me, and Emily is in school. I am glad they got the road fixed. Emily would be quite a handful if she missed another day," she chuckled as she handed Alex his lunch.

"Thank you very much. So you are off to deliver eggs then?"

"Yep," Sylvia smiled, as she waved, and said goodbye. "We'll be back soon. Enjoy your lunch Alex, and we'll see you later."

"Yes ma'am, see you later boss lady." Closing the door, he pulled up a seat near the boiler and dug into the bag. He ate the sandwiches and drank a cup of coffee. After a cigarette and a short rest, he went back to painting. For some reason, the painting did not bother him as much as he thought it would. He had painted a few times in his life, and each time he hated it with a passion. Now though, it seemed different. Perhaps because he was doing it on his own and there was no one nagging him.

Boss man wasn't kidding about those fumes. I feel like I've guzzled a quart of whiskey, he thought as he stepped outside and looked to the sky. He took the opportunity to rest and puff on a cigarette. It didn't seem to help, so he tossed it on the ground and stepped on it.

"Should never have started that habit," he said to himself as he turned and went back inside.

He found his thermos of coffee and poured himself a cup, grabbed a cupcake from his bagged lunch, and went back outside to the straw bale that was now shaded by the hay barn. He sat with a heavy sigh, *it's going to be another day before I finish. Didn't think it was going to take that long.* He bit into the cupcake and washed it down with a sip of coffee.

Although the sun was bright, it was not that hot, and he felt his hands grow cold. He rubbed them together as he stood and walked over to the stack of wood. Loading up an armful, he entered the hog barn, and tossed the wood on the floor in front of the boiler. Loading it up, he warmed his hands as he stared into the orange glow. He decided the rest of the painting would have to wait. He would finish it tomorrow. Besides, it would not be long before Kent was home and another day on the farm would end.

Finding an old ice cream bucket, he filled it a quarter of the way with gas so he could rinse out the paintbrush and took it outside. He washed his hands clean of the paint that covered them and rinsed the brushes. Satisfied that they were clean, he returned to the barn and stoked the boiler one more time. The warmer it got, the better the paint would dry through the night.

The nausea he felt earlier finally subsided, and he felt good. He was unsure if it was the paint fumes and the buzz he got or if he genuinely felt good. He turned off the blower fan and waited for it to stop whirring before he finally left the barn. The painting would be finished tomorrow. Once that was out of the way, there was still the matter of cutting down the cedar tree. Kent still had to point out the tree to fall. Indeed, there was some tough work ahead.

Chapter 12

On the Halloween weekend, after receiving his pay, Hudulak made his way into town. By the time Sunday rolled around, he was feeling the effects of two nights of boozing it up. Still groggy and nauseated he made his way back to the Townsend farm. Kent noticed immediately how hung over his help was, and chuckled.

"Well, boss man, as you can tell, I'm pretty beat up. I drank more than I should have and ate very little."

"I could tell. I hope you'll be ready for work tomorrow?"

"I will be. A good night's sleep is all I need. I won't be drinking for a while. I even threw out my smokes so I won't be smoking either." Hudulak sipped from the cup in his hand. He had consumed so much alcohol in such a short time that his hands shook. Setting his cup down, he put his head in his hands. He was grateful that the kids and Sylvia were gone. To church, he assumed. "Is everyone at church?" he asked.

"Emily and Richard are. Sylvia and Jack are over at the neighbors getting some milk and cream. We're going to churn some butter today."

"Just the thought of it makes my stomach sour. Not sure, I like butter. It always seems pretty tasteless to me."

"I guess it is all in how you make it," Kent pointed out.

With feeling so sick, Hudulak decided he should have a bath and clean up. Maybe that would make him feel a little better. He rose from the table on wobbly legs. The few steps to the bathroom made him feel even queasier. Looking in the mirror, he shook his head. He looked terrible and smelling his armpits, he realized he smelled even worse. Twenty minutes later, cleaned and shaved, he lay on his bed. In a few minutes, he was sound asleep. He woke when Sylvia knocked on the door to ask if he would be eating.

"Alex, do you want to have some supper tonight?"

"Yeah sure, I'll be right there." He still was not feeling well, but food in his stomach might be a good thing. "I haven't eaten much lately. Thank you for waking me, boss lady."

"It will be ready in about ten minutes," Sylvia said as she closed the door and began setting the table. It was only 4:00 o'clock, but Sylvia liked to have dinner finished by 5:00 o'clock on a Sunday. That way, they could all spend a bit more time together before the start of a new week. By 7:00 o'clock, Hudulak returned to bed. He slept through until Monday morning when he awoke refreshed and feeling his usual self. He was ready, for another long workweek.

In the weeks that followed, he worked diligently, and before he knew it, everything was ready for winter and the piglets began arriving. He and Kent travelled to Creston once a week, returning each time with a set of twenty. Five trips and five weeks later, it was early December when the Townsend farm once more echoed with squealing hogs.

From then on, Hudulak's job was to keep the animals fed and clean. On a daily basis, he cleaned the stalls and laid down new straw, and was tasked with keeping the barn at a constant 72 degrees. Heat lamps at night helped with this, but during the day, the only thing keeping the temperature constant was the boiler. It ate through the fuel like a rabbit eating lettuce. Hudulak stoked it every half hour. He spent more time doing that than all the other jobs.

Much of the time, all he did was sit and stoke the fire. From time to time, he would make a couple of rounds up and down the barn corridor to check on the hogs. It was an easy job during the winter. There was less to do and more time to do nothing but daydream. Hudulak did a lot of that. He often sat down and plotted things in his head. He thought about how he could get away with rape if he ever had the opportunity. It always aroused him in different ways. He was not stupid, and knew how wrong it was. Still, his desires had been, ignited many times when he thought about sex with Sylvia or even Emily. "That is so wrong," he said beneath his breath as he closed his eyes and shook his head.

Looking out the barn window, he noted the snowflakes as they danced their way gently to the frozen ground. It did not matter to him. It was warm and cozy by the boiler. The piglets were quiet for a change, and he daydreamed a little more. Christmas was only three weeks away. He knew he was welcome to spend it with Townsends, but he felt awkward enough sitting with the family. It would be twice as awkward spending Christmas with them. Nope, he needed an alternative.

The thought of returning to his roots up north did not sit well with him either. He really had no use for his alcoholic sister or nagging mother. He did have friends in that area though and spending time with them was more appealing. He had three weeks to think about it.

Rising from where he sat, he made another trip down the barn corridor and checked on the piglets. No sooner did he make his way to the end before the piglets made a ruckus that was both eerie and unpleasant.

"Shut the hell up you stupid pigs! I haven't any slop for you. Eat what you have."

He shook his head as he made his way past the occupied stalls. He could hardly wait for the day to end. Not that it had been long; rather it had been unproductive. Lazy days were the worst. They always made his mind wander to places he did not want to go. All he could do was sit and think, and he was tired of doing that now. His mind constantly drifted to the upcoming Christmas holiday, and all the nonsense that came with it. The Townsend children were showing their excitement every day. They were asking for this and begging for that; or, at least, that is how he saw it. Perhaps, if he had grown up with parents that loved their children as the Townsends loved theirs, he would have a different opinion about the whole thing. For him, Christmas meant little there was nothing he liked about it.

Stepping outside, he loaded his arms with a stack of wood. The snowflakes sporadically came and went, and a cold wind blew from the northwest. He shivered as he looked into the wind. *One week it is warm, and the next it is cold. Not sure which I like best,* he thought as he made his way back inside. He tossed the wood to the floor, knelt down, and opened the boiler. The crimson and orange coals danced to life as oxygen filled the airtight heating unit.

There, that'll keep the flames alive and the hogs warm, it could turn out to be the coldest day so far. It makes me wonder what January will bring.

Cold weather had never bothered him much, but this winter he could feel the cold bite at his hands and face as never before. He did not know why it was that way. He had lived in some of the coldest climates, and it hadn't bothered him then. Making his final rounds, he checked on the temperature and cleanliness of the stalls. Every time he walked down the corridor, the piglets came to life, and the silence of the moment was always ruined.

I'm going to take pleasure in putting bullets in your heads next fall. Damn pigs anyway.

Satisfied that the stalls were decently clean and the temperature suitable, he strode back to the barn foyer to his makeshift lunch table. There was coffee in his thermos, and he poured himself a cup. With so little to do, he felt more like a shepherd than a farm hand.

Chapter 13

On December 18, he received his monthly pay. He was excited to get it early, and booked a bus ride back up North where he decided to spend his two-week Christmas vacation. He planned to spend it with some old friends rather than with his family.

The Townsend children were thrilled when Christmas day arrived. They received all the gifts they wanted, including an expensive doll for Emily. She had wanted the doll since last Christmas. Finally, she got her wish. Tears welled up in her eyes as she tore off the Christmas wrap to reveal the doll in its box.

"Richard, Jack look, I got my dolly!"

She held the doll close to her as a mother holds a child.

"I can't believe I got my doll! I am so happy. Thank you so much Mommy and Daddy. I thought I would never get to hold her," she snuggled it a little closer.

"I'm going to name her Belinda."

Just then, Richard jumped up and down.

"I got my toy trucks and even some farm animals! This is the best Christmas ever! Thank you. Thank you!" he hollered as he continued to jump up and down.

Jack ripped through the presents Sylvia handed him like a bear ripping through an old, rotten stump looking for ants and grubs. Christmas wrap covered the living room floor in an array of different colors and shapes. It was indeed a memorable occasion, and the best Christmas ever. There was no doubt about it.

"I'm sure glad you guys like your presents," Kent said as he handed Sylvia a little tiny box.

"This one is for you."

"Oh Kent, you didn't have to."

"Yes I did. Now open it up," he said, with a smile. "I picked it out for you a long time ago."

Sylvia, slowly unwrapped the tiny box with surgical precision. Inside was a golden Angel pendant and a gold box chain. Tears welled up in her eyes and rolled down her cheek. She had wanted that necklace forever, but had not expected to get it. It was quite expensive and elegant, something she thought she could only dream about, but there it was in all its glory. She looked over to Kent with tears in her eyes.

"What? You don't like it," he teased.

"I love it, Kent. How did you know I wanted this?"

"A little bird told me." He looked over to Emily and winked.

"Well, that little bird sure knows a lot," she wiped her tears away, and leaned over and kissed him softly on his cheek. "Will you please help me put it on?" she asked as she drew the chain around her neck.

"I would love to." Kent gathered the two ends together and snapped the clasp in place. "There, it looks beautiful on you," he said as he kissed the nape of her neck.

"I will wear it with honor and pride. Thank you so much Kent." She wiped another tear away from her eye. Then, reaching beneath the tree, she fished out another box and handed it to Kent. "This one is from all of us."

"Thank you very much." Kent shook the box. He always did that with Christmas presents. "Hmmm. Now what could this be?" he smiled. "I think by the sound of it, it is a new harmonica or pipe," he looked over to the children who were sitting in a circle admiring their new toys, coloring books, and clothes. "So, am I right?" he asked of the children.

"Right about what," Emily turned to face him.

"Weren't you listening?" he was smiling. He knew that they were too enthralled with their own presents to care about his, "You know," he shook the box again. "Am I right about what is in this box?"

"What do you think is in it?" Richard queried.

Kent looked over to him with a smile. "By the sounds of the shake, I think it is a new harmonica or maybe a pipe."

"You must have been cheating, Daddy, or saw it before it was wrapped," Emily spoke up, with a giddy smile.

"No I didn't. I would never do that. I have magic ears that can hear everything," he joked. "Just like last night I heard the Reindeer on the roof. I listened real close, and I think Santa might have hid a few more presents in the corner behind the tree. You better take a look."

The children were ecstatic as they all turned in unison and looked under the tree's droopy branches to the back corner. Sure enough, there were three more presents.

"You do have magic ears! There are presents back there," Richard pointed.

"You guys better dig them out. Be careful not to knock the tree down though."

"I'll get them. My arms are the longest," Emily said as she reached in behind and gathered the few presents.

"They are from Santa Claus!" she said, with excitement. "This one is for Jack," she handed the present to her little brother. Jack took it from her with his eyes as large as saucers. "This one is mine," she set it on the floor beside her. "This one," she struggled with it for a moment, "is for you, Richard."

"Open them up. I want to see what St. Nick brought you." Kent had not opened his present yet. He was waiting for the children to finish opening theirs first. The look on their faces as they ripped through Santa's presents was the best present of all. Kent and Sylvia looked at each other with twinkles in their eyes. Richard and Jack were beginning to tear the wrappings off the last presents.

"Wait," Emily said as she crossed her arms. "You haven't opened your present yet, Daddy. Open yours and then we'll open ours."

Kent looked over to Sylvia, and the two of them chuckled. "All right sweetie, I'll open it up." Inside was a brand new kerchief and, of course, a new Harmonica. It was not just any Harmonica. Kent's jaw dropped. "A Hohner!" he exclaimed. "I can't believe it is a Matthias Hohner. Where in the world did you ever find one of these?"

It was like the one he had played when in Italy with the 1st Infantry, which he had lost during a skirmish. It had broken his heart to lose it because it once belonged to his grandfather. Now he held the same make and brand in his hand. Tears pricked at the back of his eyelids as he began to play 'Silent Night'. The children and Sylvia listened to the rhythm and hummed along. It was a touching moment for everyone.

Finishing the song, he set the Harmonica back in its box and using his new kerchief wiped his eyes. "Thank you for such a magnificent gift. I never thought I'd ever hear the sweet sound of one of these again. You all made my day. Thank you." He excused himself and made his way into the bathroom.

There, he looked into the mirror as memories of the war palpitated, his mind. He never spoke about his time there and he had no intention in doing so. Instead, on those occasions that he did think about it, he preferred to be alone. Today he was not going to let those horrible memories ruin Christmas. He wiped his tears one last time, put on a happy face, and returned to his family around the Christmas tree. "So, what did Santa bring you guys?" he asked as he sat down.

The children all spoke at once, and Kent could not hear a word of it. Instead, his thoughts drifted back to the time when he enlisted. Sylvia saw the distant look that now formed on his face.

"Is everything all right Kent?" There was a moment of silence. "Kent," she repeated. "Is everything okay?"

"Huh, oh yeah, I'm fine. I was reminiscing about last Christmas," he fibbed. He looked at his children. "Do you remember last Christmas?" he asked, to cover up his own distraught feelings.

"Yeah, last Christmas was fun too," Emily, stated.

"I think this one is better. Jack and I got everything we wished for," Richard said.

Kent smiled. "I am happy to hear that." He added tobacco to his pipe and took a long draw from it. "Well, if all the presents have been found and unwrapped and you are all content with what you got, then I'd say this Christmas day will always be remembered as one of my favorites."

"Mine too," Emily stated. "I got Dolly," she pulled the doll in close to her heart. "I got some new clothes, two books and some arts and crafts stuff, too. We must've been good because I think Santa spoiled us a bit," she teased.

She knew there was no Santa Claus, but her younger siblings believed and she was not going to ruin it for them. She looked subtly at her parents sitting on the couch and winked at them. Richard and Jack were none the wiser as they continued to play with their toys. Thirty minutes of family chitchat passed them by. Finally, Kent rose from the couch.

"I guess I better go and check on the hogs," he looked at his watch. "They are probably expecting their slop by now."

"And I should get busy with getting the turkey prepared for the oven. Emily, do you want to help?" Sylvia asked as she made her way into the kitchen.

"Do I have to?" Emily asked. She was having too much fun with her doll to want to stop.

"No, you don't have to help. Maybe you and your brothers could clean the living room up a bit, and when your dad comes back in, we will have some Christmas cookies and cocoa. How does that sound?" Sylvia removed the turkey from the fridge.

"Okay, we'll do that, right guys? We can have cookies and cocoa when we are done. It won't take us that long. Come on Jack help Emmy and me. If you want cookies and cocoa, you have to help too," Richard handed his little brother a handful of Christmas wrap. "Put this in the

Christmas box. It isn't ripped, and mom keeps the good stuff."

Jack took the handful of colorful paper and darted to the box on the floor that held the old wrap from years gone by.

"I put box," he said as he slid across the floor in his socking feet as he had seen Richard do a hundred times. At the same time, Emily was beginning to get up and Jack slammed into her, smashing his mouth into her head. A loud cry echoed, and Sylvia came running. The first thing she saw was both Emily and Jack sprawled out on the floor. Blood trickled from Jack's bottom lip, and Emily was rubbing the side of her head.

"Oh my God! What happened?" she asked as she swiftly came to their aid. It was hard for Richard to contain himself. It all looked so comical to him, but he managed to explain.

"Jack bumped into Emmy and knocked her down."

"Are you okay, Emily?" her mother asked, with concern.

"Yes Mom. I'm okay, but I think Jack is going to have a fat lip." When Emily sat up, and Jack saw that she was okay, he stopped crying. Not even the small amount of blood that trickled down his chin concerned him. Instead, he ran to Emily and hugged her.

"Emmy," he said as he hugged her, "I slip and fall."

"That's okay, Jack. I'm all right," Emily hugged him back.

"Now go with Mommy and get your face cleaned up."

"Face not dirty," he sulked.

"Yes it is Jack. Now come with me and we'll get you cleaned up." Sylvia took him by the hand and into the washroom. She dampened a washcloth and gently washed the blood from his chin and lip. Jack fought her the whole time.

"Come on now, Jack, let Mommy finish. I have to see that split lip of yours." Finally, Jack relented, and Sylvia was able to clean his face and wound. "How does that feel?" she asked as she put some salve on his lip. "You are certainly going to have a fat lip. You have to learn to be more careful Jack. You and Emily could have been hurt badly. So be careful from now on, okay?"

"I slip."

"Yes you did, but you and Emmy are okay," Sylvia said as she patted him on the bottom and sent him back to playing. "There, now to get back to what I was doing," she softly said, as she looked in the mirror and straightened her hair. Back in the kitchen, she continued preparing their Christmas dinner, and began boiling water for their morning cocoa.

Chapter 14

Before they knew it, summer was upon them. Hudulak settled in remarkably. He learned his job well. Kent was clearly satisfied with his work, and knew he would not have been able to raise the hundred hogs without him.

Emily, on the other hand, could not stand to be near him. She didn't feel safe when Hudulak was around, but she never understood why. He would look at her, and it was as if she could look into his soul, and knew that he was an evil man. She didn't tell anyone about her feelings and instead she simply avoided him whenever she could.

It was a day like any other day, hot and muggy. Everyone was busy. The kids were outside playing; Kent was getting ready for the afternoon shift, and Sylvia was making a pie in the kitchen. Suddenly, the dog started barking.

"What is all the fuss about?" Sylvia asked as she looked out the window. She was surprised to see the Smiths pull up.

"Well hello there," Sylvia yelled. "It is so lovely to see you both, come in."

The Smiths were long-time friends of the Townsends. They were one of the first couples they met when they first came to town. Kent and Sylvia had gone to the bar for a drink, and the Smiths, knowing they were unfamiliar faces, asked them to join their table. It was an instant friendship among the four of them. "I'm sorry it's just going to be the kids and me here today. Kent is about to leave for work."

There was a loud scream. It was Emily. "Mommy, Mommy, help. I've cut my leg!"

Kent and Sylvia ran outside. "Emmy, what happened?

"I tripped and fell on this rock. My leg hurts, Mommy." Sylvia looked.

"Kent, I think she needs stitches. We have to get her to the doctor." Sylvia darted back to the house and phoned the doctor, and said that she was on her way with Emily. Since

Kent was on his way out the door to go to work, he suggested that Sylvia and Emily go into Fruitvale to the clinic with the Smiths. Kent decided that he would follow in his car, thereby saving an extra trip to town.

Mr. Smith, seeing that Hudulak was left by himself, asked if he would like to come along.

"Sure, I'll come along. Maybe we could pick up a case or two of beer," he suggested as he climbed into the back seat.

While Emily was being cared for, Hudulak and Mr. Smith, not wanting to sit around and wait, headed over to the Liquor Store and picked up a couple of cases of beer. They returned to the clinic as the doctor was finishing up with Emily's stitches. A few minutes later, they all headed back to the farm.

It was the evening of July 30. Hudulak and Mr. Smith popped a beer open as soon as they could. As they continued to drink, and the hours went by, Sylvia, knowing how men got when they were drunk, offered coffee and sandwiches to help clear their heads.

"That would be really, really good. It's already almost eight o'clock and we could use a snack," Hudulak slurred as he shuffled the deck of cards they were playing with. "Who is its deal?" he asked with a slur as he began handing out the cards.

"Must be yours," Mr. Smith said, with a chuckle.

"It is too, by Christ. All right, this is five-card stud. Nothing is wild like women." Hudulak trailed off as he looked at Sylvia who was now bringing the coffee and sandwiches. With a weak attempt at slapping her on the behind, he almost fell from his chair. Sylvia rolled her eyes in disgust. She set the plate of sandwiches and coffee pot down. She slapped his hand away, "I think it is time for someone to settle down and drink some coffee."

"Oh, c'mon now, I was funning with you."

"It isn't appropriate, and I don't appreciate it," Sylvia scolded as she sat down. There was an eerie feeling in the room and an awkward silence.

"Don't stop playing cards on my account. I don't want to spoil anyone's fun. Come on deal me in," Sylvia said as she poured herself a coffee and took one of the sandwiches. "Go ahead you guys have a sandwich and coffee. It'll make us all feel better."

"Thank you, Sylvia," Mrs. Smith replied as she too poured her husband a coffee and handed him a sandwich.

"Thank you, love," Mr. Smith responded as he took the coffee and sandwich.

"They sure look good. Thank you kindly for making them Sylvia."

"It wasn't a problem."

"Never is a problem serving another man is it?" Hudulak said, as though he were on another planet.

Mr. Smith looked over to him and shook his head. "That'll be enough talk like that. Show some respect."

"Ah, I suppose you are right. Sorry ma'am."

"Now have a sandwich and coffee. It'll clear your head some," Sylvia said as she pushed the plate of sandwiches over toward Hudulak.

"I guess cards are done for the night," Hudulak replied, with little enthusiasm.

"Yeah, let's call it a night. Sylvia probably wants to relax a bit before she hits the hay. What do you say? Do you want to come into town with us? I wouldn't mind a few more beer." Mr. Smith was saying this out of concern for Sylvia. There was no way he was going to leave Hudulak alone with her, at least, not while she was awake. Maybe if he took him away for a bit, when he dropped him off later he would simply go to sleep.

"I dunno. Got a hundred hogs to feed in the morning, I guess I wouldn't mind a few more beers though."

"Go ahead, enjoy the rest of the evening Alex," Sylvia said, knowing what Mr. Smith was doing.

"I'll take the baby for the evening too if you folks want to have some fun. I don't mind babysitting."

"Thank you so much Sylvia," Mrs. Smith began. "She's asleep now, and I certainly wouldn't want to wake her. Anyway, I'm not sure it is a good idea for her to ride back to town with these two drunks," she teased.

"Drunk? We aren't drunk. Not yet, anyhow," Hudulak responded with a drunken slur.

"Will be though, eh," said Mr. Smith, with a chuckle. "Yeah, thanks Sylvia for offering to babysit. Maybe you will join us?" he looked toward his wife.

"Not on your life, I'd rather go home and sleep. You two yahoos can go on without me," she replied, jokingly.

"Ah, that is probably best," Hudulak waved his hand through the air. "Looks like it'll be just you and me, Mr. Smith. I'm all for that."

"Okay then c'mon let's go."

The Smiths said, "Goodnight" to Sylvia and kissed their daughter goodbye.

"We'll be back tomorrow to pick the baby up. Thanks again, Sylvia," Mr. Smith said.

"Don't mention it. Go out and have a good time, the baby will be fine with us."

They finished what was left of their beer, and after Hudulak had a couple of aspirins, the trio headed back to town. During this second trip, Hudulak fell asleep, and woke as they arrived at the Smith's house to drop off Mrs. Smith. Mr. Smith and Hudulak decided to go into Trail to see what was happening at the bars. They went to a couple until finally they found one with enough excitement.

"Wow, a live band, let's stay. Maybe I will be lucky enough to get a few dances in with a girl," Hudulak said.

It turned out that they had so much fun they stayed until closing. Mr. Smith, being the responsible one when out on the town, knew when he had to slow down, but Hudulak was not ready to quit. He wanted more. He talked Mr. Smith into looking for a bootlegger to get more beer. It took a while to track down someone selling booze at that time of the night. Finally, though they did. The two of them drank a couple right away as they began making their way out of Trail and back to Parksiding.

"Beer tastes pretty good eh? I don't drink too often, but when I do I like to tie one on," Hudulak said as he guzzled a half bottle in one gulp.

They continued to drink as they made their way to Fruitvale. They travelled along the old Columbia Gardens route back to the house. Having a good time and relaxing, the pair took their time in driving back to Parksiding, drinking the entire way as they drove. When they arrived at the Townsend residence, the family dog began to bark like mad.

"Shut up you mangy dog. You're going to wake the household up," Hudulak yelled out the car window as it came to a halt. Stepping out, he retrieved what was left of his share of the beer and bid goodnight to Mr. Smith. He made his way into the house, set his beer on a counter, and proceeded to bed. He would get a couple of hours of sleep if he were lucky. Not long after he had gotten comfortable, he heard the children wake and make a ruckus.

"Give me some blanket, you blanket hog," said Richard. Jack handed more of the blanket over and fell asleep. Hudulak got up and made sure the two Townsend boys were asleep and covered. For one reason or another, he stumbled into Sylvia's room where Emily was sleeping with her. He had it in his mind that he would check on Emily since she hurt her leg earlier that day. He would not normally have gone into Sylvia, and Kent's room, it was common sense. That night though all common sense was out the window, drunk as he was did not care. He stood and watched her sleep until Sylvia woke.

"Alex, what are you doing in here?" Sylvia questioned with concern.

"I wanted to come and make sure Emily was okay after she cut her leg so bad."

"She's fine, get out of here, and go back to bed," Sylvia said with trepidation, she felt a sense that he had been watching them both.

He left the room and made his way to his own. As he lay down, he heard the baby cry. Getting up again to check on the baby, he stumbled over something as he made his way back.

Sylvia woke up again. "Alex, what the hell are you doing *now*? Get the hell out of here you drunken asshole."

"I came to check on the baby because she was crying."

"I can look after her on my own!" yelled Sylvia.

He tried to ignore her but the more she yelled the angrier he grew. He began to get a little dizzy, and Sylvia continued to yell at him. "Shut up or I'm going to slap you across the puss. That'll straighten you out you stupid bitch."

"Get out of here. Get out of here right now Alex!" She was angry by this time. "Go on, get out of here!" Sylvia continued yelling at him and demanded that he return to his own room. This in turn caused Emily to wake up. "Now look what you've done. You woke up Emily."

Emily looked around in confusion, her eyes as wide as saucers. "Mommy, what's going on? Why are you and Alex yelling at each other?"

"Cause your mothers a bitch, that's why." He felt a rage begin to grow inside him, and he hauled off and backhanded Sylvia. Emily began to yell at him as well, telling him to leave her mother alone. Without skipping a beat, he twirled around and smacked her across the face too. They were both screaming now, and the baby was crying hysterically with all the noise around her.

His mind raced with the hatred he had for women. He recalled being, struck by his mother for hurting his own sister. He did not know why his mother beat him, but she had. His only recollection of that event was that he had spread the little girl's legs too far apart.

One can only speculate whether he was just changing her diaper or planning to assault her.

His rage now out of control, he tore out of the room and grabbed the first thing he could get his hands on, which happened to be a ball-peen hammer. Returning with the hammer in hand, and with the might of Thor the Thunder God, he threw it at Sylvia. It bounced off her head and smashed into the wall, plastering the wall with some of Sylvia's hair and blood.

As she screamed, he retrieved the hammer and continued to beat her with it until she was quiet. Not even the blood that spattered his face and covered his hands made him slow down. Emily watched in horror. She was screaming and pleading for him to stop, but his rage was out of control.

He turned now, looked at Emily, and with one violent swing from the hammer put a hole in the front of her skull. Blood and pieces of hair and bone splattered the walls with each blow that followed. Everywhere he looked, he could see a sea of red, as blood from both his victims pooled on the floor and soaked into the mattress and bedding. A more sinister thought now conjured up in his mind as he began ripping their clothes off. Their nude and contorted bodies aroused him, and he propped up their buttocks with pillows, and raped them as they died from the wounds, caused by the brutal beating.

As his rage began to subside, he looked at what horror lay before him. It was a scene found only in the movies. He saw a reflection of himself in the mirror. He was soaked with blood and sweat. Realizing the havoc he caused, he quickly covered the bodies. He was thinking clearly enough to cover his victims with blankets. He began to realize what he had done, and he hurriedly dashed into his own room, where he lay down for a few minutes, wishing it were all a dream.

After he lay there and contemplated his ghastly act, Hudulak rose, and went to the bathroom to clean himself up. He washed his hands and face, changed out of his blood-soaked clothes, then made his way into the kitchen where he rolled himself a smoke, as though nothing was out of the ordinary.

He took money from a coffee can that the Townsends kept in a cupboard, and made his escape by stealing the family car. He knew he had to get away; he had to flee. He didn't know where he was going to go as he made his way onto the highway. So preoccupied with what he had done that everything seemed as a blur. As he came out of the daze with his thoughts, he found that he was on his way towards Nelson.

While driving, he was making a plan. He would go through the Nelson tollbooth, across the orange bridge, then ditch the car and catch the ferry, and head home to the prairies of his youth. If he could get that far away, he might get away with the murder and rape he knew he had committed.

Beads of sweat covered his brow as he drew closer to the bridge and tollbooth. Constantly wiping his face with the sleeve of his shirt, he knew he needed to calm down, so as not to bring attention to himself. If he were caught, he knew he would be going to prison for the rest of his life.

He wiped the sweat from his brow one last time as he approached the tollbooth that would lead him across the bridge and that much closer to the Balfour ferry. Beyond that, he hoped, would be his freedom. As he drove through the tollbooth, he produced a hand full of pennies to pay for the toll.

"Here you go, sir. Sorry it is only a bunch of pennies, but I've had some hard times lately and pennies is all I have," he said, nervously as he handed the man the round copper pieces.

"Money is money," the toll officer said, although there was something about the man that didn't seem right and made him suspicious. If he were having hard times as he claimed, why was he driving such a nice car? He took the handful of coins, waved the man on and as the car drove past, he quickly wrote down the car's description and license plate number. His keen eye would ultimately lead to Hudulak's capture.

With the tollbooth behind him, Hudulak thought he might be in the clear. He had made it that far, and now he kept his eyes peeled for an old logging road where he could ditch the Townsend's car. Finally, he found one and parked the car a quarter mile off the main highway. From there it would be an easy walk.

Even in this disturbed state, he had the presence of mind to know that he had to ditch the stolen car. He gathered the few items that he had and walked back the way he had come. Beginning to relax a bit and thinking he was in the clear, he realized his head was screaming with pain. Remembering that he had seen a store nearby, he headed in that direction. Making the distance, he walked up to the counter, and purchased two bottles of Aspirin.

Not every day did people request, two bottles of Aspirin. This threw a red flag up immediately for the store clerk. Reaching for the bottles, she set them on the counter. She watched as the man counted out small change to pay for them. Not only did she note his seemingly distraught frame of mind, but she also noticed what looked like blood in his hair. Hudulak had changed his clothes and cleaned up, but not to the greatest lengths he could have, that was obvious. He also seemed fidgety. As he left the store, the store clerk called her co-worker.

"Did you see that man that was just in here? He seemed to be a wreck, and I think I saw blood in his hair. Do you think I should call the police?"

"I saw him too and thought the same thing."

"I'm going to phone the cops. Something is not right about him. I have never seen him before, and he was walking." She picked up the phone and called the police. They told her that they had heard about the same man from the officer at the tollbooth.

"Is he getting on the ferry?" the officer asked.

"Yes, I think so," she replied.

With the information received, the officer dispatched a car that was on the Riondel side of the ferry landing. Hudulak continued on his way, swallowing the aspirins as though they were candy. He had to wait a half hour for the ferry before he could board and get out of the area. By then, the aspirin were taking their toll on him, and he looked and felt even sicker than he actually was. *If I can catch this ferry without anyone taking notice I will be free,* he thought.

He was not thinking about the evidence he left behind at the house, his blood soaked clothes, his fingerprints on the hammer. The police were already on their way to the Riondel ferry landing. Hudulak had no way of knowing that. Had he known that the police would be waiting for him at the Riondel ferry landing, he would have gone the other way, up towards Kaslo.

He started to get excited as he saw the ferry pull up. When he boarded he thought he had it made. Forty-five minutes later as the ferry pulled up to the Riondel dock, he noticed a police car sitting there, as though waiting for someone. *What now?* He thought, as he stepped off the ferry, a police officer approached him.

"Excuse me, sir. Stop right there!"

Hudulak looked at him. "Are you talking to me?"

"Yes." the officer said, "we need to ask you some questions."

"What about?" asked Hudulak. His nervous anxiety was as evident as the blood in his hair.

"You were seen paying at the tollbooth with coins. It was phoned in as being of a suspicious nature. Where is the vehicle you were driving?"

"I, I, umm, I wasn't driving anything. I walked on from the Balfour side." Sweat was starting to bead on his forehead, and his breathing became rapid.

"Are you okay?" the officer asked." Trained, as he was, he noted the sweat, and that the man seemed distant. "I'm going to phone an ambulance to get you to the hospital."

"No, no, that's ok," Hudulak, said. "I'm fine."

"I don't think so. We're taking you in," said the cop.

Hudulak knew then that he had better start acting. If asked anything, he would not remember. The other officer approached now as well, and the two police officers helped him back to their waiting car. With Hudulak now settled into the backseat, the lights on the car began to flash, warning others that there was an emergency. When the final car unloaded from the ferry, the police vehicle boarded. No one else was, allowed on, and the loading gate closed. The warning horn on the ferry sounded, and the ferry headed back to Balfour.

Hudulak was, rushed to the Kootenay Regional Hospital. As the police pulled up to the emergency door, the first officer stepped out, opened the back door of the police car, and retrieved their passenger from the backseat. The driver opened the emergency side door and immediately requested assistance from the medical staff on duty. They came running with a wheel chair, and the officers helped them get him seated. "We think he is overdosing. He has been rambling on about aspirins that he has taken, and seizures he claims to have had," said the officer as the nurses wheeled, him into a room where they and interns attempted to pump out his stomach, a process that was usually easy.

However, Hudulak vomited as the nurses tried to insert the throat tube used to empty out his stomach. They cleaned up the expelled vomit and tossed it in the garbage. Only three flasks with Hudulak's stomach contents were, saved. There were no remains of the hundred or so aspirin that he claimed to have taken, nor were there any signs of the reported epileptic seizure he claimed to have had the night before. It was, of course, something that he fabricated.

Richard lay in bed, which seemed like hours, holding Jack until the first rays of sunshine came over the mountain. He knew Hudulak had left the house by now, but knew not to get out of bed until daylight.

"Stay put Jack I'm going to see Mommy for a minute. Whatever you do, don't move." Jack was young, but he knew this time to stay put. Richard, slowly, his heart pounding out of his chest, made his way into his mother's room. He wasn't prepared to find what he found. The walls of his mom and dad's bedroom were crimson with blood. His mother and sister were motionless, pulling back the covers he saw pieces of hair and flesh matting the pillows. He knew that something terrible had taken place and cried out in horror! "Mommy, wake up! Wake up Mommy. Please!"

There was no movement, or sound at all, his mother's face and silky brown hair lay in a pool of coagulating blood. Her face was so badly beaten he hardly recognized her. Getting ready to run from the room, he heard the baby behind him in the playpen. He had forgotten all about the baby. *I have to get Jack and the baby out of here as fast as I can,* he thought. "Come on baby, I've got you." It was by pure instinct that he knew what to do. He ran to his room and with fear in his voice yelled to Jack. "We have to go right now."

Jack didn't have any clothes on, but Richard didn't care. He knew he had to get away immediately and get away fast. Something terrible had happened, and he needed to get help. It was quite a distance to their nearest neighbor, and he was exhausted by the time they made it there. He had carried the baby the entire way.

All three were crying. Richard was crying because he remembered what he saw and was horrified. Jack was crying because he was naked, cold, and scared. The baby was crying because, she was being bounced around by Richard who was trying to go as fast as his and Jack's little legs would carry them.

The neighbor, luckily, was up early to get her husband off to work. She happened to look out the window. She could not believe what she was seeing. There was Richard with the two other children. Startled, she abruptly dropped what she was doing and rushed to the children. "Richard," she asked, "what happened?" By this time, Richard was crying so hard he could hardly speak.

"Mommy is dead! Mommy is dead!"

Confused and aghast at what she heard, the neighbor brought the children into her house where she called the RCMP and another neighbor. With the children somewhat settled, the neighbors made their way to the Townsend farm. Approaching the front door, they began calling for Sylvia.

"Sylvia, are you here? Sylvia, can you hear us?"

No reply came. Finding the front door locked, they used the back door to get in, calling the whole time. The house was silent. From what they saw at first, it looked as though there was nothing wrong at all. There was nothing to suggest that any foul play had taken place. The front room and kitchen were both neat and tidy. Except for a bit of tobacco on the kitchen table, everything seemed normal. When they checked the bedroom however, they discovered the horror that had taken place.

Lying on the bed were two bodies, mostly covered by blankets. Sylvia's head was showing along with her and Emily's feet. The neighbors were sickened to see all the blood that splattered the wall. "Look at the blood! It's everywhere! Oh My God! What in the hell happened here?" They were in total shock at the horror they were seeing.

Both Sylvia and Emily's facial features were, smashed beyond recognition. "I have to get out of here, I'm going to be sick," one of the neighbors said. She ran outside in time to vomit on the grass. The other neighbor followed close behind, both women were aghast at what they had seen, who could have done this horrific crime?

One of the women described that Sylvia and Emily both looked like raw meat. Sickened at what they discovered, they cried and talked amongst themselves as they waited for the RCMP to arrive. It seemed like forever to the neighbors, but, in reality, it was only a short time.

"What is going on?" the officers asked the one woman who seemed to be in less turmoil. They could see that the she was horrified.

"Inside, inside," that was all she could get out, her voice was almost inaudible.

"What's inside?" one of the officers asked. It was obvious that the two women were too distraught to answer questions, leaving them to sit on the grass. They cautiously entered the Townsend house. At first, they could not see anything, but as they made their way through the house and into each room, they soon discovered what they were looking for. They had both been on the force for years, but they had never come across anything as ghastly. "I have to get out of here," one of the officers said "I need a minute of fresh air," he gasped as choked back a mouthful of vomit.

"Me too," said the senior officer. The two of them went outside to regroup. It took some time for them to come to terms with what it was they were dealing with, *a homicide*. Radioing ahead to dispatch, they requested an ambulance and the coroner. They took hundreds of pictures, and while they were looking for evidence to get an understanding of what had happened, they found the bloodstained hammer.

"This has to be the murder weapon," the senior officer said. "It has hair and flesh all over it. Grab me a bag so we can save it for evidence." As he searched the murder scene, the other searched the house for more evidence. In the boy's room, he found a set of blood-soaked clothing. They soon learned that they belonged to the Townsend's hired hand, one Richard Alexander Hudulak.

Chapter 15

While the police continued with their investigation of the murder scene, and they were bagging, tagging, and documenting the evidence, one of them called ahead to Kent's work to ask them to keep him there for a while longer. His boss told the officer that Kent had worked a double shift because they were short, staffed, and that he had already left for home. The senior officer thanked him and hung up the phone.

"Mr. Townsend is on his way home," he began. "We have to stop him, before he gets here, come on, let's go," he said as the bodies were carried out of the house and placed in the ambulance to be transported to the hospital, morgue.

As the police drove toward the gas station to stop Kent, he passed them. Slowing down they turned around and headed after him, by now though Kent was turning down the road that led him home. Seeing the ambulance, he sped his truck up as dust billowed behind him. Finally making the distance he threw open the driver side door and quickly raced toward the house, paying little attention to the neighbors standing on his lawn.

"Kent, stop! You can't go there!" one of the neighbors yelled, trying to stop him.

"To hell I can't," he said as he ran into the house. Looking around, he saw the disarray near his room, and made his way there. Seeing the bloodstained mattress, and the blood, smeared wall, his knees buckled, and down he went. "What happened, where is Sylvia, where are the kids?" he pleaded as tears welled up in his eyes.

The officers who tried to divert him from making it home, now pulled up and ran into the house, "Mr. Townsend, please, let's go outside so we can talk," said one of the officers, as he helped Kent up.

"Where is my family!" he screamed. They gently explained to him what had taken place and that they were

141

doing all they could to find Alex. Kent went into a deep shock and collapsed on the lawn. The officers helped him up again and sat him down in the police car, and one of the paramedics administered a morphine shot to calm him down.

With the murdered victims on their way to the morgue for autopsies and all evidence gathered, the police dropped Kent off at a neighbor's house, and requested that they call the police station once he came around.

It took some time to inform Sylvia's family in Alberta about the murders. At first, they thought that only one murder had occurred. They learned the magnitude of the situation on the evening news. Back then, communication was poor, and news travelled slowly. When Sylvia's family heard what had happened, they came immediately to be with Kent and the boys. No one wanted to believe what had happened.

Sylvia's sister June, along with Kent made their way to view the bodies at the morgue. At the discretion of the medical examiner they were allowed to view Sylvia, but not Emily due to the barbarity of how she died, she had been, brutalized and was beyond recognition.

There was not, much known about Hudulak, other than the fact that he had applied for the job at the Townsend farm through a letter of correspondence, which proved that he could read and write English. He claimed he could not do either at the time of his arrest. No one knew what kind of monster Hudulak truly was. *He hid it well.*

Tests proved that, at the time of the murders, Hudulak had not suffered an epilepsy seizure like, he had claimed. Yet the experts claimed that he might have suffered *just that* on the night of the slayings. This is quite the contradiction. It is possible that his epilepsy symptoms grew less frequent and may have stopped altogether as he reached adulthood.

During his youth, Alex Richard Hudulak, learned how to manipulate both the system, and law enforcement agencies using his epilepsy as a reason for loss of memory, and things he did. Petty crimes, assaults and the like, he blamed on his epilepsy and alcohol abuse. He often claimed that he was drunk or had suffered one of his fake seizures when accused of committing a petty crime. He was a liar and a manipulator. He was going to do his best to fool them all again.

Kent and his surviving family were going through hell while Hudulak played the game. Justice certainly was not being served rather it was being manipulated by a psychotic killer. For four years he was, psychoanalyzed and in treatment, a-far cry from the harsh prison environment he knew he deserved.

He spent four months only in the Oakalla prison. Court appointed doctors, and psychologists examined and found him in a psychotic and suicidal state. Their recommendations were that he needed hospitalization in a mental hospital and that he was unfit to stand trial. He was mentally insane, they said. Hudulak though, was far from insane he was simply manipulating the system.

They quickly moved him to Essondale Mental Hospital, and not a Federal prison where he belonged. For four years following his initial arrest, Essondale Mental Hospital was his home, when all along it should have been a prison.

In November of 1963, Hudulak was able to stand trial. He appeared before a judge and jury, surprisingly, by those in attendance he was, acquitted of both murders due to an insanity plea, and was, sentenced to strict custody in a mental hospital at the pleasure of the Lieutenant Governor. He received a conditional discharge on December 13, 1974, and in 1977, an absolute discharge from custody landed on his lap.

He spent less than twenty years in an insane asylum for the murders he committed. Many saw this as unjustifiable, and truly, it is a dark stain in our Justice system when clearly, he should have imprisoned in a Federal prison.

Perhaps he would have paid for the vicious attack with his own paltry life. Crimes involving rape and murder of woman and children are as unacceptable today as they were then.

Protective Custody does not always protect those that commit these types of crimes. Other inmates often brutalize those convicted. There are documented cases of criminals who paid with their own lives. Many thought that is what should have taken place. Hudulak should have paid for his crimes either at the hands of the law, or at the hands of the lawless.

During the preliminary hearing, Hudulak showed no remorse. When asked by the presiding Judge if he had any questions, his answer was always 'No'. In the minds of many then and now, there is no doubt whatsoever that Hudulak knew, exactly what it was he had done that fateful night. His actions alone should have been proof enough that while he committed the murders he was of sound and mind. It goes without say, that ignorance and pity played a part in Hudulak being hospitalized, and not sent to a life behind bars.

Two months after his sentencing to Essondale Mental Hospital, an IQ tests along with EEG testing were conducted, it was discovered that he had an IQ of 82, which put him in a borderline group of people barely able to handle the first years of secondary school. However, with a score like that, he certainly did know right from wrong. The EEG testing used alcohol and Metrazol in hopes of activating an epilepsy seizure. This test failed to produce any such seizure.

A similar test had been done in 1954, five years before he committed the murders, to see if he was free of epilepsy. It too failed to produce any hallucinations or delusions, which would have been, expected from someone suffering from epilepsy. The conclusion is that his epilepsy was well under control. It is possible that, during the night of July 30, 1959, he was suffering from an epileptic reoccurrence. However, it is more plausible that he was not.

Although Hudulak was not a brilliant man, he was smart enough to cover up the acts he had committed. During the interrogation, he claimed he couldn't read or write English that well, yet he had been seen reading newspapers. As well, he had written the letter to Kent in his own handwriting that ultimately helped him gain employment on the Townsend farm. How could it be that the law courts and the RCMP could not see through Hudulak's lies? Could it have been due to the small town mentality?

In years since, Fruitvale has not been immune to vicious murders. To the people who lived in the area in 1959, it was a massive shock and undoubtedly the worst homicide to date. The violent murders that Hudulak committed were so brutal and shocking that perhaps the RCMP couldn't see the truth, the truth that Hudulak was everything society said of him, *except insane.*

There are numerous reasons why Hudulak managed to fool those in authority, and land himself in an institution as opposed to a prison cell. Perhaps the investigation of the murders and the investigation into Hudulak's past and mental state were flawed. Ultimately, though, his success boiled down to his creativity in playing the victim, and using his epilepsy to explain what happened to Sylvia and her daughter.

There was no evidence whatsoever that Hudulak suffered a relapse or seizure so severe that it would cause him to act as he had by murdering and mutilating his victims. His defense was simply another one of his ploys. He claimed that he and Sylvia were having consensual sexual relations. This idea stems from his sick own fantasy. Sylvia was not promiscuous, but Hudulak was certainly trying to make it seem that way with the lies that came out of his mouth when, he was interviewed, by the RCMP. Sylvia was unable to speak for herself and so he could say whatever he wanted, and he did. There was no relationship sexual or otherwise, between Sylvia and her slayer.

Hudulak was an employee, but that is not all that he was. He was a vicious murderer, rapist, liar, and phony. Being the wretched and pathetic man that he was, he deserved to die of old age behind bars steel. Eighteen years, in a mental hospital hardly accounts for the lives he destroyed.

Kent tried to remain strong during this time, and continued to provide for his two sons. It was all he could do to get out of bed in the mornings. *If only I had died along with them,* he often thought. *I'm not sure I can go on with my life or if I want to. I have the boys to consider. How am I going to get through my days and be a parent to them the way they need?* Thoughts and questions such as these were a constant battle for him.

Not many men today could handle what he while the killer of his wife and daughter was sitting in a mental hospital and not the Federal prison where he undeniably belonged. That thought alone would render many men into seclusion, alcoholism, and depression, making them incapable to provide for themselves or others. Kent, though, was a hard and just man, with a strong and honest character. He knew that he needed to move on, if not for himself, then for his two sons, but knowing and doing were two different things.

Chapter 16

During their marriage, before Hudulak's murderous rampage, Kent and Sylvia fought with the sadness of the loss of three babies due to illness and stillbirths. How they had cherished sweet Emily, whose life was, ripped away at the hands of a vicious and psychotic killer. He had lost one woman to another man as he fought for the peace and freedoms we all cherish today. Now he had lost a wife and a daughter, at the hand of someone he had trusted to employ. The guilt was overwhelming for him. *If only I hadn't hired him. If only I could have seen through this man. How could I have not known?* He often thought, but there were no answers.

Kent now had to fight his own war on a daily basis, not in combat, but with what life had brought his way, and what a struggle it was. He faced adversity, disappointment, and death many times before 1959, which only a man of honor with the courage to accept life, could have endured. He was honorable, courageous, and sincere. Yet, justice failed him by sending the man who killed his wife and daughter to a mental institution rather than a penitentiary. His whole world was crumbling. Where was, the justice, and the peace of mind, that he surely deserved?

It was only Kent's employer, Cominco, whom supported him through those trying times. They paid for the funeral in its entirety. Including the matching coffins, he wanted to bury his loved ones in. He was not a rich man, and his employer knew this. Any extra money the Townsend's had was spent on Hudulak's wage. If it had not been for Cominco, the matching coffins would have been beyond his reach. It was only due to Cominco's generosity that he found solace.

Being the proud man that he was, he insisted on repaying the money to Cominco through his wage. The funeral turned out as Kent had planned. The sun was shining. The sky filled with the bluest of blues as though the victims had summoned the color. White roses and daisies covered the coffins from top to bottom. There were so many bouquets sent from well-wishers, the Church where the funeral took place looked like a floral shop. It was filled to capacity with friends and family. Those who couldn't find chairs, of pews to sit on, stood outside to show their respect.

People that the Townsend's didn't even know came from miles around and grieved alongside him. Kent was grateful and amazed for the love he received. Deep down, he knew that Sylvia and Emily were, blessed by all.

Chapter 17

In time, the youngest boy lost all memory of the murders until he was in his early 30's. It was a terrible tragedy to have witnessed. It is no wonder that the youngest erased it from his childhood memory. Richard, however, would never forget that traumatic day. No one knew how he dealt with his horror. He did not speak of the murders again.

Kent, on the other hand, dealt with the deaths by slipping into deep shock. It was all he could do every day to get out of bed to face the days without Sylvia and Emily. Even though he fought in Italy during World War II in the 1st Infantry, those he had seen die in Italy were trained to fight and trained to die.

The brutal deaths of his wife and daughter were senseless killings. The training he received while enlisted may have helped him deal with the loss to a degree. He hid the pain deep, the same as he did when his comrades who fought with him fell. His wife and daughter, though, were not comrades. They were his life. Just like Richard, he did not speak of the murders.

As the days turned into weeks, he returned to work. After weeks of being alone without his sons, they were finally coming home. He had missed them terribly. He wondered how he was going to care for them, and wondered how they were coping, since he could hardly manage.

When Richard and Jack arrived, the three of them embraced each other. He looked at their little faces as he held them tight, and sadly realized that they would never be the same. Their eyes had lost their sparkle. Even Jack, who was only two, knew somehow that things were different.

As time faded and days came and went, Kent went through four sitters before hiring a young woman as a live-in nanny. He met her one day while delivering eggs to neighbors. Her name was Edith, and she had lost her husband a few months earlier. She had been married a little over a year. She was from Alberta but was visiting her late husband's parents for a few days. She was a special kind of woman, always looking out for other people. Her mother-in-law introduced her to Kent knowing he needed a sitter and that Edith needed a job.

It wasn't long before she moved in with them as a live in nanny. She shared the room with the boys, and the boys felt protected. They had nightmares for quite some time, but she was always there beside them as soon as they made a peep. She would hold them tightly until they were once again fast asleep.

As far as she and Kent were concerned, she knew she had to get on with her life, and he seemed to be what the doctor ordered. She was attracted to him. He was exceedingly handsome with a smile that melted her heart. The only thing was that smile did not appear very often, but when it did, her heart would skip a beat. Kent enjoyed her company, liked having her around, and hoped this arrangement would go on indefinitely. Perhaps love was in the air once more for Kent; God knew he deserved it.

For almost a year, she worked for Kent, avoiding his bedroom at all cost. She was afraid to enter it, and sickened to know that the walls were still, splattered with the blood from Sylvia and Emily. Kent made it abundantly clear that no one, was allowed in his room and she did not dare to disobey him. Her job was to maintain the rest of the house and to be a Nanny for Jack and Richard.

During this time, Kent continued to suffer from his loss. At times, he was overbearing and demanding. The life he once knew was over for him, and he was now easily angered. It was long time before, Edith began to mother the two boys and developed a deepening attraction to Kent, and he too began to feel the same toward her. Part of his heart was telling him to be loyal to Sylvia, but another part was saying it was time to move on. He was torn between these choices.

Eventually, Edith moved to a small community called Miette Hot Springs and began her life anew. Weeks passed, and Kent began to feel tired and defeated. He worked extremely hard at his job, and the daily grind of running a farm and raising his sons was taking its toll. He realized the worth of the woman whom he had let get away. His sons missed the companionship and motherly love she provided. They begged him to get her back.

After some pleading and a few too many cold suppers, Kent finally agreed with them, and they went to Miette Hot Springs to ask her to return. He didn't know what he was going to say to her, but he had to convince her to come back, for the two boys, if not for him. *Perhaps it was love.*

Chapter 18

Returning to her role as a surrogate mother, as time went by she also took on the role of the new Mrs. Townsend and the love between them blossomed. In 1961, a year after Kent and Edith married the Townsend family grew. A daughter was born to the newlywed couple. It was a glorious occasion for Kent. After all that happened to him in his life, as he looked down upon his beautiful daughter, he felt blessed. Could this be the change that, he needed? Could the birth of his new daughter fill the void? Only Kent knew the answer.

One thing was for, certain he loved that new bundle. Her golden hair and blue eyes were that of an angel. He could not believe how beautiful she was. As he held her for the first time, he broke down and cried. With all the losses he endured, he felt like he owned the world at that moment. He felt blessed. For a little while, he felt whole once again.

The boys were thrilled at the birth of their sister, and they welcomed her with a kiss on the cheek. During the days that Edith remained in the hospital, the two boys could hardly wait for visiting hours. Although, at times, the visits were short, they looked forward to every moment they could spend with their new sister.

The day mom and baby were discharged happiness enveloped the Townsend family. It was such a relief to Edith to be going home. She wanted to be in familiar surroundings with the baby. What bothered her about going home was that the baby's crib was set up in their bedroom, the same bedroom where the murders took place. She never felt comfortable in that room, but for now, she would try to be content as possible regarding the sleeping arrangements, no matter how uneasy she felt.

When the baby needed feeding at night, she didn't feed her in the bedroom. Instead, she would feed her in the living room or at the kitchen table. The less time that she spent in that room, the better, in her opinion.

It must have been as tough for her as it was for Kent to have to sleep in that room. However, Kent was set in his ways. She knew for now, this was the way it was going to be. There was no point in arguing or fighting over it. In time, she knew she would win the battle, no matter what. In order to get on with their lives and to make it as pleasant and fulfilling as possible, a definite change needed to take place. Whether or not he would have admitted it though, was another story.

Although 1961 brought with it the birth of their daughter, a happy and joyous occasion indeed, it was also the year that Hudulak received a Stay of Proceedings on the grounds of insanity in the deaths of Sylvia and Emily Townsend. Hudulak received no penalty, or charge whatsoever regarding Emily's death nor was he charged with rape. When the coroner examined the victims in the days that followed the ghastly murder it was evident that they had been sexually assaulted, before, during, or after death. It was even in the coroner's report. For one reason or another it had either been overlooked, or completely ignored by the powers that be.

A *Stay of Proceedings* meant that, for now, Hudulak would not be facing any of these charges. Kent was shocked and in disbelief. *How could it be that a man who so brutally murdered his wife and daughter be given such sanctuary?* It was simple. He had fooled them all.

Kent knew Hudulak was sane, his pleas to the fact landed on deaf ears. It was an insult. No one wanted to listen. All he could do was to accept the penalty that Hudulak received, as pathetic as it was. The only good thing was that Hudulak was somewhat detained.

With the court proceedings over for the time being, the Townsends tried to get on with their lives as best as possible. However, the disappointment Kent felt hung over him like a black cloud for years. Little did he know that Hudulak was given daily passes, he had gotten a job working the Essondale farm because he was such a model patient. He was free to work and go wherever he chose. For a few days, he studied the grounds then one day, he simply walked away from the Essondale farm. When his escape was discovered later that day the RCMP were immediately informed, and in turn, they informed Kent.

He felt like he had been hit by a truck when he answered the phone that day. Hearing the news he wanted to throw up, he was weak, and his body trembled.

"Mr. Townsend, we will be doing everything we possibly can, to get him back into custody, and when that happens, and it will, I assure you, we will call."

Kent hung up the phone, sat down and cried. He was terrified that the son of a bitch would come back, and if he did, he would shoot him. For six day's fear enveloped the valley. Finally, Kent got the call. "Mr. Townsend, this is the RCMP. We have Hudulak back in custody. He was picked up in Alberta, your family is safe."

"Thank you for letting me know, I was prepared to shoot him, if he showed up here," Kent made clear.

"Well, let's hope that never happens," the officer understood Kent's anxiety and desire to kill the man who had killed his wife and daughter, but he also understood that such action would only mean a charge of murder against him. "Everything is going to be okay, Mr. Townsend. Everything is going to be okay," he repeated to console him.

Happiness for Kent was only a nine-letter word, and for now, it meant little. Things would change as life went on, but the memory of Hudulak's crime was like a constant news flash in his mind. There was no justice for Kent or for his murdered wife and daughter.

Time went on.

With his family growing, he knew he had to have a bigger house. He had some options. One was to sell the farm and move on. That was out of the question because he had worked too hard building up the paradise he and Sylvia had created. He was not going to let Hudulak's acts send him running away. He had not run away from anything, and he was not about to start now.

Another option was to build a new house and tear down or burn down the old one. That too was out of the question. Financially, he could have rebuilt, but there was more to it than that. Again, to him, it seemed like running, and he couldn't let the house go. He just couldn't give up what he and Sylvia had created together.

In order to keep the house, increase its size, and change the setting, he built a new foundation and moved the house to a new location on the property. He pondered this idea for some time until finally deciding that would be the right decision for them all.

He did most of the labor by hand, with a shovel and pick. It was not an easy feat at all, but it needed to be done. In Kent's mind, hard work did not hurt anyone. His sons helped by picking up rocks and piling them at the new site. He figured that the work was good therapy. It took their minds off what had taken place a few years earlier.

As for their childhood and the things children of their age did, Richard and Jack missed playtime. They had daily chores that they were expected to do. Work was work. Their age did not matter. Kept busy by their father, the two little tykes worked every day. Edith would sometimes step in and ask Kent to take it easy on them.

"Kent they are just little boys. Please don't push them so hard."

"Oh for God's sake, they can handle it. Hard work is good for them. It gets their mind off things."

"No, Kent. It gets *your* mind off things. That is what it actually boils down to, isn't it?"

Grumbling, Kent would walk away. He did not talk about his feelings and he was not about to start now.

On occasion, Richard and Jack would grab a couple of homemade hockey sticks and slap balls, pucks, and apples back and forth. This was a playtime for them. For a few moments, they were kids. Then the work would start again. It was a hard life made even harder by Hudulak's rampage. To grow up in the house where two lives had been taken certainly did not make for a happy childhood.

The boys, however, were suppressing the horrors that had taken place. The work they did on a daily basis was becoming a normal way of life. It was far from normal though. Children of their age should not have to work as hard as they did. In addition to the murder that Hudulak committed, he also affected the lives of the two children. Their happiness suffered a great deal. There was no way to tell what lasting effect the ordeal contributed to their lives.

Chapter 19

The years went by, and Kent and Edith raised their three daughters. They hid the tragedy from the girls so as not to worry them, but they heard the story more than once. They knew that a terrible murder had taken place in the house where they lived and grew up.

Kent and Edith tried their hardest to stay together, and they succeeded for years, but in the end, they called it quits and divorced. They sold the farm, which was another blow to Kent. He moved to a small town nearby.

He was an amazing man in that no one ever knew how his heart ached. He was always out dancing and smiling. His love for dance and music got him through the last years of his life. He even had a few ladies along the way for companions. His last hours of life were at an old time fiddlers' party, where surrounded by friends, he suffered a fatal heart attack at the age of 74.

As for Edith, she lives on with all the memories of those years, glad to have her three daughters and her grandchildren to keep her life as busy as she can handle. She loved Richard and Jack as though they were her own. The boys called her Mom and she called them her sons.

Perhaps Kent should have channeled his anger differently, but it always seemed to be Jack, who was the target of his anger. The boy tried his hardest to impress his father, but something would always go wrong. Once more, he would find himself at the end of a yardstick, or in some kind of confrontation with his dad.

Nobody guessed that the boy's troubles were indeed due to the carnage and horror he lived through. From his point of view it seemed, everything that went wrong, was either due to his failure at one thing or another, or that he was simply a target for his father's anger. There were times when things were good and other times when Hell was unleashed. Jack wanted to have as normal a life as possible. However, due to one man's murderous rampage, he was affected in many ways.

He paid for that man's crimes by being the vent for his father's anger. He paid for it with all the sleep he lost over the years due to the nightmares. He paid for it by the loss of ties that bind a family together. How unfair that must have been. He didn't speak up to express what he remembered of the crime. He was brought up to 'speak when spoken to'. If no one else spoke of the event, then obviously, he was not to speak of it either.

By the time he was twelve, he suffered a great deal more than the man who murdered his mother and sister. He felt slighted by society and rebelled against authority. His anger was not much different from the anger his father had. It only differed because he was a kid, a kid who had witnessed Hell up close. Eventually, it led him to be sent to a foster home.

As Jack grew up, he began to show signs of antisocial behavior. By age ten, he would act in ways that could not be controlled by discipline alone. His behavior was aggressive and verbal, towards his classmates and other students that attended his school. It could not be determined as to why he acted as he did.

He suppressed and forgot the earlier events, but there was anger inside him that he could not control. He wondered where the anger came from. He knew that his father was mean at times. A lot of the time, it seemed to Jack that his dad always lashed out at him, never Richard. Jack's anger was deep, cold, and callous. He even scared himself sometimes.

One fateful day at school, one of his outbursts was so violent that Edith was, called to remove him. She had no idea what she was going to do. Kent and Jack had been butting heads for a long time, and she knew that Kent would be furious when he found out what Jack was doing. When she arrived at the school, she was shocked to see Jack. His eyes were wild, and he was in a fit of rage. She had never seen a rage in Jack before.

It was suggested that he be placed in the hospital under care. The principal had called in a psychologist after he had phoned Edith. The doctor had arrived a few minutes earlier and had seen Jack's behavior.

As soon as she arrived at the school, the school psychologist sat her down. "I'm afraid your son needs some counseling. I would like to admit him and see if we can help him. He has a lot of built up anger inside. Can you tell me a little bit about him? I understand his mother and sister were murdered some years ago."

"He was only two years old when that happened. I'm not sure if you have heard the story or not."

"I have," the doctor replied, as solemnly as he could.

"There has never been any mention of the murders in the house since it happened and being so young, we don't think he remembers. Please, for Jack's sake, do not tell him what happened either."

The doctor agreed not to say anything. "However, it is possible he knows more than we think. A child can remember things long after they have happened. They go into a type of regression, and it can be the simplest thing that brings it all back to them. It is hard to say at this stage if this is the reason for his outbursts today. Still, I think counseling him in that area is going to be the only solution, to prevent this type of thing from happening again. Jack is a strong child, and it would not take much for him to hurt someone, especially in a fit of rage as we have seen here today. I would like to admit him for observation for a couple of days at the least."

"I wouldn't know what to tell his father," Edith lowered her head as though she were going to cry.

"Tell him the truth," the doctor put his hand on her shoulder as a way to comfort her. Edith nodded her head.

159

She knew that was the best thing. Making up a false story would only anger Kent more.

For a week, Jack remained hospitalized. His behavior while there was listless and uncooperative. No specific reasons for his outbursts were, discovered, but the doctors believed that they were, related to the horror of the murder of his mother and sister. At one point while he was in care, the neurologist whose care he was under, wanted to give him shock treatment, but Edith refused to give consent.

"That is the last thing you will be doing to my son. He is not crazy! Have you any idea what this boy has been through in his life. He lost his mother and sister to a brutal murder, and you want to give him shock treatment. No way!"

It was obvious to her that her stepson's behavior was due to the tragic loss and vicious murders he witnessed as a child. There were those that would have argued that case, being as the boy was so young when it happened. However, being the mother that she was, she felt she knew the reasons for his outbursts, and shock treatment was out of the question.

Counseling in her opinion would have a better outcome. Kent was still against that, just as he was in the first few years after the murders took place. Now, eight years after the fact, he believed the young boy was simply misbehaving and that it had nothing at all to do with the tragic loss of his sister and mother. Kent believed that a better course of action was the iron fist of discipline.

This began a downfall between a father and son. He ran away many times as a child only to be, brought back to his 'hell on earth' as he called it. The older he got, the angrier he was toward his father and vice versa. It seemed that they could not stand each other anymore. Kent was angry because Jack was always misbehaving and Jack was angry because it seemed he could do nothing right.

He was eventually, put into foster care until he was of legal age, and during this time, he seemed to have gained the tools he would need to lead a productive life outside of foster care. Still his angry outbursts when things didn't go the way he thought they should, made it very hard for him to hold steady employment. Truck driving he learned to be his niche in life. As a truck driver, he was free to work at his own pace without anyone telling him what to do. He had enough of that growing up.

He was married and divorced twice, but finally found his forever sweetheart. On weekends, he would go home to her. His home life was complete and he was happy and content with how his life had turned around. Sadly, he died suddenly at the age of 53 due to a heart attack.

Richard, on the other hand, showed no aggressive behavior whatsoever as he grew and became a man. He was soft spoken, friendly and well behaved. Many of his classmates growing up in the 1960s and 1970s remained in school until grade twelve. He too, would have graduated had it not been for an arbitrary rule of the school that saw him expelled.

Kent, although upset at this, did not react physically. "If you intend to live under this roof you either go to school or go to work because you are not living here for free," that is all Kent said and he meant it.

Two days later, Richard left home and found employment as an Assayer in Sparwood, B.C. Time came and time went and another move found him in Terrace, B.C. where he attended welding school, and in the process received his high school diploma. Throughout the few months of schooling, the valley of his home kept calling him back. He would never forget the tragedy that had taken place, but he felt he belonged there. Eventually, he returned to the home of his youth. He ran his own welding business Sparky's Welding for many years, and his knowledge of the welding trade grew, he gained a reputation as a hard worker, and in the years that followed gained employment with Cominco. Preferring the security, that Cominco could offer, he sold his business. Tragically, he died at the young age of 55 from cancer.

www.ingramcontent.com/pod-product-compliance
Lightning Source LLC
Chambersburg PA
CBHW060251050426
42448CB00009B/1612